T0165492

The World Before A Watching Church

The Biblical Motivation for Living the Christian Life

DAVID M. ROSSI

WESTBOW
PRESS
A DIVISION OF THOMAS NELSON

ISBN: 978-1-4497-2070-4 (e)
ISBN: 978-1-4497-2069-8 (sc)
ISBN: 978-1-4497-2068-1 (hc)
Library of Congress Control Number: 2011932924

WestBow Press books may be ordered through booksellers or by contacting:

WestBow Press
A Division of Thomas Nelson
1663 Liberty Drive
Bloomington, IN 47403
www.westbowpress.com
1-(866) 928-1240

"Scripture quotations taken from the New American Standard Bible®, Copyright © 1960, 1962, 1963, 1968, 1971, 1972, 1973, 1975, 1977, 1995 by The Lockman Foundation Used by permission." (www.Lockman.org)

Printed in the United States of America

WestBow Press rev. date: 8/31/2011

Contents

PART I. THE WORLD AND THE CHURCH   1

PART II. THE RETURN TO THE FOUNDATIONS   39

**PART III. THE EXHIBITION OF THE CHRISTIAN
FAITH**   127

❧ Acknowledgments ❧

I would be remiss if I were not to mention that this work would not have been made possible without the opportunity afforded to me by my dear wife, Sheryl. Apart from her support and her loving encouragement, this project would never have been accomplished.

Also, I wish to thank those who read the manuscript and provided thoughtful and Biblical insights: my brother, Joe Rossi, of Otter Creek, Michigan and my pastor Dr. Bradley Burrell, of Marion, Ohio.

I should also mention our dear friend Gail Anderson, who was only able to critique a portion of the manuscript, before being called to be with the Lord, forever.

My prayer is that my children (Christopher, Jennifer and Sally) and my grand-daughters (Annika and Kersten) will realize the same confidence, as I do, in the plan that God has for all who trust in Christ as Savior.

And to all who read this text, may they be challenged to faithfully do the work that is before us as Christians – to think, speak and live Biblical truth into our culture.

❧ Preface ❧

The following study is addressed specifically for those who have trusted in Christ as their savior. When it comes to spiritual phenomenon, the unbeliever neither understands nor accepts "the things of the Spirit of God."[1] Only the believer in Christ has the indwelling Holy Spirit Who teaches, convinces and convicts the Christian in his moment-by-moment walk of faith.

It is imperative for the believer to be rightly related to the Holy Spirit in order to obtain maximum benefit from His teaching ministry. The directive stated in 1 John 1:9 for confession and cleansing of sin should be exercised prior to any instruction of the Word of God.

---

[1] 1 Corinthians 2:14

❧ Introduction ❧

In 1971, Dr. Francis A. Schaeffer wrote a book entitled: *"The Church Before the Watching World."* In the opening paragraph he stated:

> As Christians we say we believe in truth and in the practice of truth, and yet we face much untruth in the visible church.[1]

In the past 30 plus years, the invisible or universal church[2] (which includes the visible church that Dr. Schaeffer spoke of) has failed to heed his counsel and is still faced with a plethora of doctrinal error. His advice was well founded in the inspired text of Scripture, and yet his directives appear to have fallen upon the deaf ears of the universal Church.

He further stated that:

> As the bride of Christ, the church is to keep itself pure and faithful. And this involves two principles which seem at first to work against each other: (1) the principle of the practice of the purity of the visible church in regard to doctrine and life; and (2) the principle of the practice of

---

[1] Schaeffer, Francis A. (1982) *The Complete Works of Francis A. Schaeffer,* Wheaton, IL: Crossway Books, 4.115

[2] "The invisible church is Christ's spiritual body, which is *His exclusive work,* while the local visible church (es) are *a work of Christ's disciples on earth"* [emphasis his]. Geisler, Dr. Norman, *Systematic Theology,* Bethany House, Minneapolis, MN, 4.65

an observable love and oneness among *all* true Christians regardless of who and where they are. [emphasis his][3]

Despite the efforts of television evangelists, the mega-church movement, the charismatic movements, bible schools and seminaries, regardless of their denominational affiliations or non-affiliations, little has been accomplished to put into practice the two principles Dr. Schaeffer challenged the 20th Century Christians.

By applying these two very basic, essential principles in our daily walk of faith, the challenge for the 21st Century Christian now is to prayerfully acknowledge the failures of the past and ask God for the strength and divine guidance to go forth into the world and represent Jesus Christ as He has intended for us.

It is imperative for us to understand these failures. The author has taken care to insure that this study is not a vehicle to criticize any particular denomination or individual or organization thus placing blame for the dilemma in which the Church finds itself today. Yet it is obvious that the world no longer looks to those who are supposed to be imitators of Christ before a fallen world. We have repulsed them. They have gone their own way believing that God and Christ are simply relativistic ideas for those who are weak in mind. We are obligated to convince them by our words and reinforce them by our actions that God does exist and that He indeed sent His Son to reconcile the world to Himself. Our culture speaks volumes to its decadence: the broken lives and families; politicians and judges who have lost their moral compass; rampant crime and evil, driven by an entertainment industry that glorifies the criminal element and devalues human life. People are beginning to accept this as normal. And yet we Christians have the answers for modern man to bring him back from the depths of despair and to provide him with direction for a life that could be rich in meaning and purpose.

The intent of this book is twofold: to appeal to pastors, seminary professors and Sunday School teachers to explore the Biblical solutions that the visible church can employ to regain its footing within the culture of the 21st Century; and that believers who make

---

[3] Schaeffer, 4.115

up the Body of Christ will reach their spiritual growth potential and be equipped to effectively witness for Christ in every segment of our culture. We should not be content in accepting the status quo of the Church: standing by and watching its culture self-destruct. We must convey the message of Jesus Christ, precisely as He instructed, in a unified manner.

DAVID M. ROSSI
June 6, 2011

PART I:

THE WORLD AND THE CHURCH

❧ 1 ❧

THE BIBLICAL PERSPECTIVE
OF THE WORLD

An important principle of Biblical interpretation is the study of words. Words mean something. They are the building blocks of effective communication. One needs a vocabulary to think and to communicate; therefore the Creator inspired the men who wrote the Scriptures to employ specific words and terminology in order to precisely convey everything that He desired man to know about Himself.

Bernard Ramm states that:

> Words are the units of thoughts, and the bricks of conceptual construction. Any study of Scripture, therefore, must commence with a study of words...[1]

A good starting point then would be to define the two main terms in the title of this study: the world and the Church (Chapter 2). The purpose for this would be to make as clear as possible what is meant by these terms within this present study based upon the understanding of their usage in the Bible.

---

[1] Ramm, Bernard (1956) *Protestant Biblical Interpretation* Boston, MA: W.A. Wilde Company, p.129

WORLD DEFINED

The following is a contemporary definition of the word 'world' taken from the Internet's Wikipedia Encyclopedia.

> The World is a name for the planet Earth seen from a human point of view, as a place inhabited by human beings. It is often used to mean the sum of human experience and history, or the 'human condition' in general.[2]

Webster's dictionary defines the world thus:

1. a: the earthly state of human existence b: life after death -- used with a qualifier <the next *world*>
2. the earth with its inhabitants and all things upon it
3. individual course of life: CAREER
4. the inhabitants of the earth: the human race
5. a: the concerns of the earth and its affairs as distinguished from heaven and the life to come b: secular affairs
6. the system of created things : UNIVERSE[3]

The modern understanding of the word is basically the earth and the sum of mankind's experience. Note that the #6 definition in Merriam-Webster refers to the world as "the system of created things." The questions we could ask are: Does modern man truly believe in the created order of the universe? And, do they know who the Creator is? However, the Scriptures state that "the god of this world has blinded the minds of the unbelieving."[4] This being true, we as believers in the Lord Jesus Christ must recognize this opposition which works to neutralize our efforts at spreading the Gospel and glorifying Jesus Christ.

In the New Testament, the predominantly used Greek word

---

[2] "World," Wikipedia, The Free Encyclopedia, 2010, http://en.wikipedia.org/wiki/World

[3] *Webster's 7th New Collegiate Dictionary* (1965) Springfield, MA: G&C. Merriam Company, p.1030

[4] 2 Corinthians 4:4 NASB (Unless otherwise noted, all Scripture references are taken from the *New American Standard Bible: 1995 Update*, La Habra, CA: The Lockman Foundation)

translated 'world' 186 times in our English, is *cosmos* [κόσμος]. Bishop Trench explains the classical usage of this word:

> 'Ornament,' and obtaining this meaning only once in the New Testament (1 Peter 3:3), where we render it 'adorning'...from this it passed to that of order, or arrangement.[5]

It's primary usage according to the Greek Lexicon:

> In philosophical usage *the world* as the sum total of everything here and now, *the (orderly) universe* [6]

However, this word in used in a difference sense in many other passages of the New Testament (John 8:23; Ephesians 2:2; 1 Corinthians 3:19):

> *The world,* and everything that belongs to it, appears as that which is hostile to God, i.e. lost in sin, wholly at odds with anything divine, ruined and depraved.[7]

Biblical language scholars have observed *cosmos* to mean an orderly opposition to God:

> The present world, the present order of things, as opposed to the kingdom of Christ; and hence, always with the idea of transience, worthlessness, and evil both physical and moral, the seat of cares, temptations, irregular desires.[8]

Also,

> The *kosmos* (understood as the world of men) constitutes a uniform subject which opposes God in enmity, resists the redeeming work of the Son, does not believe in him,

---

[5] Trench, Richard C. (1975) *Synonyms of the New Testament*, Grand Rapids, MI: Wm. B. Eerdmans Publishing Co., p.214

[6] Arndt, W., Gingrich, F. W. (1957) *A Greek-English Lexicon of the New Testament and Other Early Christian Literature*, Chicago, IL: University of Chicago Press, p. 446.

[7] Arndt, W., Gingrich, F. W., p.446

[8] Zodhiates, S. (2000, c1992, c1993). The Complete Word Study Dictionary: New Testament (electronic ed.) G2889. Chattanooga, TN: AMG Publishers.

and indeed hates him (Jn. 7:7; 15:18ff). It is ruled by the prince of this cosmos (Jn. 12:31; 16:11), i.e. the Evil One (1 Jn. 5:18).[9]

The common idea in all these definitions is 'order.' There is order in our world. However the New Testament writers make it clear that this order is at odds with anything divine, of which we are commanded to avoid being stained by (James 1:27), becoming friends with (James 4:4), and influenced by its lusts (1 John 2:15-17).

THE RULER

The significance of this word 'world' describes the culture in which we live. It is a culture that is cleverly structured. While most people believe it is the sum of all of its parts, all the varying ideas and personalities, all of the different races and sexes, the Scriptures state otherwise. They reveal that there is a ruler of *this world* (John 12:31; 14:30; 16:11), and that "the whole world lies in the power of the evil one" (1 John 5:19). This 'evil one' is a real person, the ruler of this world, Satan, "the prince of the power of the air" (Ephesians 2:2).

In the wilderness temptation account the devil stated to Jesus:

> "I will give You all this domain and its glory; for it has been handed over to me, and I give it to whomever I wish" (Luke 4:6).

This is an undisputed statement, boldly asserted by Satan himself of his controlling powers over the world.

Lewis Sperry Chafer sums it up succinctly:

> The *cosmos* is a vast order or system that Satan has promoted, which conforms to his ideals, aims, and methods. It is civilization now functioning apart from God – a civilization in which none of its promoters really expect God to share, who assign to God no consideration in respect to their projects; nor do they ascribe any causativity to Him.

---

[9] Joachim Guhrt, "earth", in *New International Dictionary of New Testament Theology*, Colin Brown, Ed. (1986) Grand Rapids, MI: Zondervan, 1.525

This system embraces its godless governments, conflicts, armaments, jealousies, its education, culture, religions of morality, and pride. It is that sphere in which man lives. It is what he sees, what he employs. To the uncounted multitude it is all they ever know so long as they live on this earth. It is properly styled *the satanic system*, which phrase is in many instances a justified interpretation of the so-meaningful word, *cosmos*. It is literally a *cosmos diabolicus*.[10]

He adds

It is this, the specific study of what is one of the greatest doctrines of the New Testament, which many worthy men have failed to pursue; and, because this body of truth is so little apprehended, the great company of believers are unaware of the enmity which the world system sustains towards God and His people.[11]

The present culture has ridiculed the idea that there is a real devil, i.e. Satan.[12] The producers of Hollywood films consistently make light of the god of this world by presenting him in various non-menacing characterizations, or in horror films as the horned, red-skinned creature carrying a trident. Of course, they have also repudiated the fact of the God who is their Creator. And the truly sad commentary is that many who claim to believe in Jesus Christ have rejected the doctrines entailing the reality of Satan and his world-wide rule.[13]

---

[10] Chafer, L.S., (1976), *Systematic Theology*, Dallas, TX: Dallas Seminary Press, 2.77-78.

[11] Chafer, 6.180

[12] The Barna Group Research: (2002, October 8) More than half of adults (59%) say that the devil, or Satan, is not a living being but is a symbol of evil. Available: http://www.barna.org/barna-update/article/5-barna-update/82-americans-draw-theological-beliefs-from-diverse-points-of-view?q=trinity+satan [2011, May 30]

[13] The Barna Group Research: (2002, October 8) Catholics (75%) Protestants (55%) hold the view that Satan is a symbol of evil. Available: http://www.barna.org/barna-update/article/5-barna-update/82-americans-draw-theological-beliefs-from-diverse-points-of-view?q=trinity+satan [2011, May 30]

THE OCCUPANTS

Two categories of people occupy the world: (1) those who believe in the Lord Jesus Christ, and (2) those under the controlling influence of Satan. There is no third possibility. This observation is based upon the absolute authority of the Word of God. Men either walk in the light or walk in darkness. John wrote: "Men loved darkness rather than light, for their deeds were evil" (John 3:19). This is true even though the Light had shone into the darkness of this world (John 1:5). We have identified Satan, the Evil One (1 John 5:19) as the ruler of this world. He is working in the background, while men go about their lives oblivious to his reign. He has blinded their eyes so that the light of the truth of Jesus Christ is obscured.

For those who walk in the light, those who have trusted in Jesus Christ as their Savior, their eyes have been opened "so that they may turn from darkness to light and from the dominion of Satan to God."[14] This was the directive that the Lord Jesus Christ gave to the Apostle Paul on the road to Damascus. It wasn't a new directive, for men throughout the ages have been commanded to seek their Creator. He has always been accessible through faith. For by faith, Abraham was accounted for righteousness, based on his belief in the revealed plan of God for his life. And so it is true for this age that men have been charged to believe on the Lord Jesus Christ and be saved.

THE PURPOSE

When we consider the purpose of the 'world,' we are actually evaluating the aspirations of the ruler of this world, Satan.[15] As already stated, his chief aim is to blind the "minds of the unbelieving, that they might not see the light of the gospel of the glory of Christ who is the image of God."[16] This statement by the Apostle Paul is a summation of the satanic activity which takes place in our culture today. Satan's intention is to instill in the minds and hearts of men

[14] Acts 26:18
[15] Matthew 12:25ff
[16] 2 Corinthians 4:4

a disbelief in the existence of the Creator and the work of the Son of God which was accomplished on the Cross. The world today ridicules these beliefs and attempts at every level (historical, archeological, and hermeneutical[17]) to disprove the truth of Christianity. This Satanic Cosmic System has infiltrated every area of society with its godless world view, including religious organizations, some of which even dare to claim to be Christ's.

THE FUTURE

The Apostle John recorded the indictment of the world: "And the world is passing away, and also its lusts."[18] Note that John states that in reality this world is in the process of passing away right now. Previously in this passage John had already asserted that the "darkness is passing away (same verb and tense), and the true light is already shining."[19]

Peter writes, echoing the words of Isaiah 40:6-8, concerning the perishable conditions of men and the world.

> All flesh is like grass, and all its glory like the flower of grass. The grass withers, and the flower falls off, but the word of the Lord abides forever.[20]

Therefore, we see that there is a temporal nature to this world and man. What becomes of them? Of Satan? The judgment of the Creator will fall upon them. In fact, the Lord Jesus spoke of this while He was still on the earth.

> Now judgment is upon this world; now the ruler of this world shall be cast out.[21]

And regarding the convicting work of the Holy Spirit, Jesus stated:

---

[17] Hermeneutics is the study of the methods employed in the interpretation of Scripture.
[18] 1 John 2:17
[19] 1 John 2:8
[20] 1 Peter 1:24-25
[21] John 12:31

...and concerning judgment, because the ruler of this world has been judged.[22]

'Has been judged' is a perfect tense verb in the Greek. According to Wallace, the perfect tense may be used to *emphasize* the results or present state produced by a past action.[23] So what Jesus was saying is that the ruler of this world (Satan) has already been judged and this judgment still stands today. When was he judged? The answer is found back in the Garden of Eden, recorded in Genesis 3:15. The Lord God said to the serpent:

> I will put enmity between you and the woman, and between your seed and her seed; He shall bruise you on the head, and you shall bruise Him on the heel.

This is not just a nice little Sunday school story. This event occurred in time, so that if you had had a video recorder you could have taped the whole incident of the Fall of Adam and Eve and the judgments that the Lord God placed upon them as well as the serpent, who is none other than Satan.[24] The judgment proclaimed was that He (Christ) shall bruise the head of Satan, to bring to an end his reign of evil upon this world. This scene demonstrates a remarkable similarity to our present day judicial trial proceedings: the judgment phase was in the Garden, the sentencing phase is yet to come.

Again, John records the final sentence executed for the ruler of this world, Satan:

> And the devil who deceived them (the nations, i.e. the world) was thrown into the lake of fire and brimstone, where the beast and the false prophet are also; and they will be tormented day and night forever and ever.[25]

There is also a judgment for all those who have followed Satan and refused to recognize their Creator. It follows Satan's judgment in

---

[22] John 16:11

[23] Wallace, D. B. (1996) *Greek Grammar Beyond the Basics*: An Exegetical Syntax of the Greek New Testament, Grand Rapids, MI: Zondervan Publishing House, p. 574

[24] Revelation 12:9

[25] Revelation 20:10

Revelation 20:11. It is called the Great White Throne Judgment. They will be judged "according to their deeds." They will be sentenced to the lake of fire, if their names are not found written in the book of life.[26]

This judgment of those living and dead will take place. It is not a science fiction or some tricky religious device to scare people to Christ. There may well be some of our loved ones in this judgment who will refuse to heed the Gospel in spite of all of our efforts and those of fellow believers in presenting the truth to them of Jesus Christ. They will love darkness rather than light, because their eyes are blinded.

CONCLUSION

It is past time for the visible Church of Jesus Christ to realize that this world, our culture, is not a very nice place. It is considered normal only because it does not vary from the norms and standards which the consensus believes to be normal. It is a very foul place because of its ruler who blinds the eyes of the world and has been doing a rather nice job of blinding the eyes of God's people. Satan does not work alone. He has his minions, his children of wrath who live indulging themselves with the lusts of the flesh and the mind (Ephesians 2:3). With Satan, they "unite as the 'world' to oppose the course of the believer."[27] But just as he is not alone in his efforts, we too are not alone. For John writes:

> You are from God, little children, and have overcome them; because greater is He who is in you than he who is in the world. [28]

The hope and assurance of the Church of Jesus Christ is that we can overcome the corruption of this satanic world system. We must take a candid look at our surroundings and become unified in our efforts

---

[26] Revelation 20:15

[27] Barnhouse, Donald Grey, (1965) *The Invisible War*, Grand Rapids, MI: Zondervan Publishing House, p. 81

[28] 1 John 4:4

to confront the 'world' according to the directives which have been given to us in God's Word on how to live in this world even though we are not of this world.

CHAPTER CHECK

1. In the past, how have you understood the word "world" to mean?

2. Explain what the Biblical writers mean by the word "world."

3. If we Christians truly believe that God is ultimately in control of His universe, then how do we explain the power demonstrated by Satan?

4. In what ways have you seen the culture ridicule the fact of Satan's existence?

5. What are the two types of people who occupy the earth? How do they differ?

6. Name some examples of Satan's attempts to blind the minds of unbelievers.

7. What is to become of this world?

ᴈ 2 ᴈ

THE BIBLICAL PERSPECTIVE
OF THE CHURCH

THE CHURCH DEFINED

Webster's Dictionary renders the word:

1. a building for public especially Christian worship

2. the clergy or officialdom of a religious body

3. a body or organization of religious believers as: a: the whole body of Christians
b: Denomination c: Congregation[1]

The first and second definitions are not used in the Bible. The third definition embraces the Biblical treatment of this word, with the exception of the church being a denomination. There were no denominations in the 1ˢᵗ Century church and so the word was never used in such a manner.

The Greek term used in the New Testament is *ekklēsia* [Ἐκκλησία]. It is a compound word literally meaning "to call out." Zodhiates further states that:

> It was a common term for a congregation of the *ekklētoí*, the called people, or those called out or assembled in the

---

[1] *Webster's*, p.149

public affairs of a free state, the body of free citizens called together by a herald.[2]

The New Testament translators demonstrate the various nuances of this word. It is translated: "the *congregation* (Israel) in the wilderness" (Acts 7:38); a lawful *assembly* to discuss social affairs (Acts 19:39); a riotous *assembly* (Acts 19:32, 41). But it takes on a technical meaning for the universal or invisible Church of Jesus Christ, "to the whole company of the redeemed throughout the present era."[3]

This is the Church which the Lord Jesus Christ prophesied to come in Matthew 16:18 (Note the use of the future tense: "I *will* build my Church"). Later, the Apostle Paul describes the Church as the Body of Christ, asserting that the Father "gave Him as head over all things to the church, which is His body" (Ephesians 1:22-23). The Biblical usage of the word Church, in its technical sense is the universal Body of Christ, consisting of those who have trusted Christ as their Savior. Further expanding this, Dr. Chafer has written:

> The deeper spiritual use of the word *church* refers to a company of saved people who are by their salvation called out from the world into living, organic union with Christ to form His mystical Body over which He is the Head… The spiritual meaning is thus seen to be far removed from mere recognition of a building which may be called a church, a congregation however organized, or any form of sectarian constituency.[4]

THE BEGINNING

The formation of the Church began on the day of Pentecost, 50 days after the Ascension of the Lord Jesus Christ into heaven. In Acts chapter 2, the Apostles and disciples of Jesus were gathered

---

[2] Zodhiates, G1577
[3] Vine, W. E., Unger, M. F., & White, W. (1996) *Vine's Complete Expository Dictionary of Old and New Testament Words* (2:42). Nashville: T. Nelson
[4] Chafer, 7.127

together in anticipation of the next event on the Divine agenda. They were expecting the return of Jesus to restore the kingdom to Israel. This event was indeed on their minds just prior to the Ascension event (Acts 1:6). However, the Lord told them (1:5) to wait for the promised Holy Spirit, who would empower them to be His witnesses "both in Jerusalem, and in all Judea and Samaria, and even to the remotest part of the earth" (1:8). It should be further noted that the means by which the Church would originate was proclaimed by John the Baptist. In Matthew's Gospel, John stated:

> As for me, I baptize you with water for repentance, but He (Jesus) who is coming after me is mightier than I, and I am not fit to remove His sandals; He will baptize you with the Holy Spirit and fire.[5]

On the morning of the feast of Pentecost this prophecy was fulfilled (Acts 2:1-13). The Holy Spirit, having descended upon them in what appeared to be "tongues of fire", filled them and enabled them to speak in various languages. This was so that they could preach the Gospel of Christ in the languages of the Jews who had come to Jerusalem for the feast of Pentecost.

As the events in the book of Acts unfolded, the disciples came to realize that their calling was not merely to the Jews, but also to the Gentiles. In Acts 10, Peter is directed in a vision to go to Cornelius, a Gentile in Caesarea, and preach the Gospel. When Cornelius and those accompanying him had received Christ they also received the Holy Spirit to the amazement of the circumcised Jewish believers who had come with Peter. Circumcision became another issue that perplexed the Apostles as they contemplated this new phenomenon of Gentiles believing in Christ. This matter was resolved at the council at Jerusalem in Acts 15, stating that the Gentile believers were not obligated to be circumcised. These events made the way of salvation equally accessible to both Jew and Gentile, a doctrine that is developed further by the Apostle Paul in his writings.

---

[5] Matthew 3:11

THE MEMBERS

The membership of the Church of Jesus Christ is made up of all who have been and will be saved in this present age. In the early days of the Church, the Apostle Paul made the assertion that it didn't matter if you were a Jew or a Gentile, all were united together by faith in the Lord Jesus Christ, and all were equal as members of the Body of Christ. This unique concept of the Church is known as the Mystery Doctrine of the Church "which in other generations was not made known" as stated by Paul in Ephesians 3:5. Although the Church had been prophesied by Jesus prior to his death (Matthew 16:18), the Mystery Doctrine of the Church was revealed by the Apostle Paul when he wrote that:

> ...the Gentiles are fellow heirs and fellow members of the body, and fellow partakers of the promise in Christ Jesus through the gospel.[6]

W. E. Vine points out:

> Gentile believers are not raised to the level of Jewish believers; both are brought out of their former conditions into the high privileges of fellowship and association with Christ.[7]

So, in this divinely appointed age of the Church, all men and women who have trusted in Jesus Christ as their Savior, regardless of race, social status, political affiliation or nationality are members of the Church, the universal body of Christ. Membership in a local church does not constitute being a member of the universal Church, for an unbeliever could be a member of a local church. It should be made clear that the commonality of all members of the universal Church is that they have all placed their faith and trust in Jesus Christ.

---

[6] Ephesians 3:6
[7] Vine, W.E. (1996) *The Collected Writings of W. E. Vine*, Nashville, TN: Thomas Nelson Publishers, 4.216

THE PURPOSE

The fundamental purpose of the Church of Jesus Christ, as Paul explains, is to glorify Him "to all generations forever and ever" (Ephesians 3:21). The members of the universal Church are saved for a specific purpose. The Christian is not saved merely to provide him with fire insurance, i.e. to escape eternal damnation. He is saved in order to serve God and to glorify Him by a faithful life. This entails a conscious moment-by-moment walk which places Him and His directives at the very core of the believer's life.

Scripture teaches that believers are to serve and glorify God as a unified body. The church is the organic union which Paul speaks of in Ephesians 4. He states in verses 4-6 that there is one body (the universal church), one Spirit (the Holy Spirit), one hope (an eternal destiny), one Lord (Jesus Christ), one faith (a cohesive body of doctrine), one baptism (the identification with the Spirit), one God and Father. Paul prefaced this by instructing believers to show "tolerance for one another in love" (v.2), and commanding them to "preserve the unity of the Spirit in the bond of peace" (v.3). We are to learn how to live in a unified manner with others who believe in Jesus Christ. This concept of unity is designed to make the body of Christ perfect or complete,[8] enabling it to serve and to glorify Him without internal conflicts. Jesus stated that in addition to the body being made perfect through its unity, this demonstration of oneness is a proof statement to the world that the Father sent the Son. Unity in the body of Christ is essential and is intended to be powerful evidence that God does exist and that the Son was sent from the Father to save men.

THE DESTINY

The church is a growing organism[9] comprised of individuals who have trusted in Christ as their Savior. Upon its completion, the Lord will return in the air to rapture His church at a time that only the

---

[8] John 17:23
[9] Cp/w Ephesians 2:21, 4:16; Colossians 2:19; 1 Peter 2:5

Father knows (Matthew 24:36). The term 'rapture' comes from the Latin *rapio,*[10] translated "caught up" in Paul's disclosure of this event in 1 Thessalonians 4:16-17:

> For the Lord Himself will descend from heaven with a shout, with the voice of the archangel and with the trumpet of God, and the dead in Christ will rise first. Then we who are still alive and remain will be caught up together with them in the clouds to meet the Lord in the air and so we shall always be with the Lord.

The Apostle Paul writes in 1 Corinthians 15:52 that at the rapture we who are dead "will be raised imperishable, and we will all be changed." He states further in Philippians 3:20-21 that this transformation of our body will be in conformity with His resurrection body. And, as already mentioned, this will be our physical condition residing with Him for all eternity.

Following the rapture of the Church, the believers will receive the rewards for faithful service during their lifetime (1 Corinthians 3:12-15 cp/w 2 Corinthians 5:9-11). After this the Church will be prepared as the bride for the marriage of the Lamb (Jesus Christ).[11]

Since our eternal hope (Colossians 1:5) and inheritance (1 Peter 1.4) are said to be stored for us in heaven and as Paul states that our Master is in heaven (Colossians 4:1) it stands to reason that our home will be with Him forever in heaven. This is substantiated by His promise prior to His death: "I go to prepare a place for you" (John 14:2).

CONCLUSION

It should be emphasized that the Church was designed to be a body of believers, serving together as a unified organization, regardless of race, color, nationality, or denominational affiliation. This is not meant to demean the importance of the individual. The individual

---

[10] Robertson, A.T., (1931) *Word Pictures in the New Testament,* Nashville, TN: Broadman Press, 4.32

[11] Revelation 19:7-9

believer still stands or falls before his Lord, and he still must make daily decisions in serving his Lord. But there are unifying elements which Paul articulates in Ephesians 4:3-6: one body, one Spirit, one hope, one Lord, one faith, one baptism, one God and Father. It is on the basis of these elements of oneness that the Church was intended to live by and demonstrate to a world without Christ, thus fulfilling what Jesus stated:

> I in them and You in Me, that they may be perfected in unity, so that the world may know that You sent Me, and loved them, even as You have loved Me. (John 17:23)

CHAPTER CHECK

1. Does the Biblical usage of the word "church" refer to a building?

2. Explain the different ways that the Scripture uses the word "church."

3. When and where did the church begin?

4. Who constitutes the Body of Christ?

5. Why is it important to understand the significant difference of the *visible* church and the *universal* church?

6. What is the fundamental purpose of the church?

7. What are the unifying elements of the church?

❧ 3 ❧

THE CHURCH IN THE WORLD

Having defined the Church in a general manner, our attention is now turned to the place of the Church in the midst of the world, i.e. Satan's cosmic system. More precisely: how is the Church to view itself and its purpose in the world in light of divine revelation.

As previously stated, the Church is the universal Body of Christ. Since the Body of Christ is on the earth, than it follows that the Church ought to be working as if Christ were present on the earth. It should be doing those things that Christ did while He was here so that His presence could be realized by those who are in need of Christ's saving work. Instead the Church is splintered, mostly because of doctrinal differences, but also because of an erroneous understanding of our wonderful position *in Christ* (Ephesians 2:6-7).

The Apostle Peter makes a statement that is well worth noting:

> But you are a chosen race, a royal priesthood, a holy nation, a people of God's own possession, so that you may proclaim the excellencies of Him who has called you out of darkness into His marvelous light (1 Peter 2:9).

The first part of Peter's statement proclaims our position as believers in Jesus Christ. We are not second class citizens of Heaven; we are declared to be royalty. No other peoples have been considered royalty in God's plan for the ages. But not only this, we are a holy nation, separated from the evil of this culture for the purpose of making known by our witness the superiority of God the Creator. It is this statement of Peter's that gives great meaning and relevance to the Christian's life in this age. In the face of an evil generation, we must rest upon the truth of our position with a full realization that we were called out of the darkness of this world and placed into His marvelous light. Not to bask in the light, but to proclaim in every corner of Satan's domain that truth and light are in Jesus Christ.

NOT OF THE WORLD, BUT IN THE WORLD

Just prior to the Lord Jesus' death on the cross, He spoke these words to His disciples:

> If you were of the world, the world would love its own; but because you are not of the world, but I chose you out of the world, because of this the world hates you (John 15:19).

Compare Our Lord's words "you are not of the world" (restated in John 17:16) with His equally affirmative statement of John 17:11: "They themselves are in the world." This is not a contradiction but a truth which every believer should fully comprehend. The underlying truth is not esoteric in its meaning, once the significance of the *world* is understood. Believers who are alive physically, live and reside in this world system which is under the control and evil influence of Satan (Ephesians 6:12). The fact that we are not of this world denotes that we now belong to God because of His regenerating work in us (1 Corinthians 6:19; Titus 3:5). When John states that "Whoever believes that Jesus is the Christ is born of God" (1 John 5:1), he is asserting that believers have a heavenly origin. And yet we are physically in this world because God has a plan for our lives that is to ultimately glorify Him.

There is certainly no denying the Biblical and historical evidences that the early 1st Century disciples of Jesus were under great testing from different segments of their culture. They were consistently at odds with the leadership of the Jewish religious system as well as the Roman government. However, when you look at the culture of the 21st Century, you see a very similar hatred for Christians who claim Jesus Christ as Savior, but for different reasons. Christians are despised because the culture has a deep-seated guilt from their rejection of the Creator and the suppression of this truth (Romans 1:18-19). The unbeliever does not want to relinquish their self-supremacy. In doing so they believe that they are the final authority for their lives and that there is no God and there is no need for God. Since they are unable to physically strike out at the Creator, they unload their anger and hatred on the Christian. They cannot tolerate the ever present reminder of their rebellion and seek every avenue which the culture offers to defeat, deter and decimate the truth of Christianity. But the unbelieving culture does not stand alone in this confrontation. Jesus tells us that Satan, the evil one (John 17:15), is a ruler of this world (John 14:30) who *has* been judged (John 16:11) and will be cast out (John 12:31).

Once we understand this principle that our new life in Christ is not of this world, we must then separate ourselves from the evil influences of this world system. This does not mean that we become monastic in the practice of our faith. It simply means that as we become more aware of the distractions of this world, we should then become more responsive to how God wants us to live, based upon His Word.

On this point Dr. Chafer writes:

> This cosmos system is largely characterized by its ideals and entertainments and these become allurements to the Christian…These features of the cosmos are often close counterfeits of the things of God and in no place does the believer need divine guidance more than when attempting to draw the line of separation between the things of God and the things of Satan's cosmos.[1]

To comprehend that our present day culture is under the evil, controlling influence of Satan is to fully appreciate the precarious

---

[1] Chafer, 2.330

position in which we Christians live today and our need for Biblical direction. We will now examine six directives from Scripture for the believer and his relationship with the world system.

LOVE NOT THE WORLD

The first directive is found in the first epistle of John:

> Do not love the world nor the things in the world. If anyone loves the world, the love of the Father is not in him (1 John 2:15).

The English translation fails to carry the full significance of John's instructions to his readers. Literally he says: "Stop loving the world." It's interesting to note that the 1st Century Christian had the same problem that we have today – an inordinate affection for the world system and the things (distractions) within the world. The love which John speaks of here is the self-sacrificial type of love, similar to Christ's love demonstrated on the Cross.

The Church today has been undertaking to heal the wounded world of all its ills: the hungry, the homeless, the un-clothed, the disaster stricken, and the war-torn. We are utilizing social and political programs to accomplish this all for the love of our fellow man. However, it is for the wrong reason. Certainly the Church should be doing these things and doing them better than any humanitarian organization. But we should be doing this for the sole purpose of our love for the Lord Jesus Christ, and to be effective witnesses for Him within this world system. The notion that we can make this world system better or to eradicate once and for all time Satan and his influence is nowhere found in Scripture as a directive for believers today.

We are also told to stop loving the *things* in the world. This would include anything which distracts us from living a moment-by-moment godly life. Any detail of life (i.e. a person, an automobile, a career, a hobby, a college class, an electronic gizmo, entertainment) that diverts the believer from their normal responsibility of spiritual endeavor, than that distraction is being loved beyond Biblical reason. The believer is then being controlled by the things of the world, and as John emphatically states, "the love of the Father is not in him." John's full meaning is that not only is there no evidence of love toward the Father but that the Father's love is not completely operational in the believer. It is a condemnation that we hold precious these temporary *things* of the world.

Are we to then shun all these *things* of the world? The point is not to shun the things of the world, but we are not to allow them to control our lives and impede our spiritual growth or to thwart the out-working of the Holy Spirit in our lives.

KEEP UNSTAINED BY THE WORLD

James wrote concerning the practice of the believer's faith; he called it "pure and undefiled religion." He states that:

> Pure and undefiled religion in the sight of our God and Father is this: to visit orphans and widows in their distress, and to keep oneself unstained by the world (James 1:27).

There is nothing worse than getting a stain on a brand new white shirt or blouse. Once it is stained much time is consumed attempting to remove the stain and to restore it to its pristine condition. But a stain by nature most often becomes stubbornly irremovable and spoils the clothing of its unsoiled status.

It is the same with believers. Once they partake of the evil vices of the world, there is a staining of the soul. If the association was favorable and appealed to the lust and the inhibitions are muted, then it will take much time, effort and prayer to rid oneself from the stain of sin.

But James gives us preventative advice: to be consistently guarding ourselves from the world influences that contradict the teachings of Scripture. These influences may range from the flagrancy of sexual immorality to the subtlety of gossiping and maligning, and when they are combined with the attitude that everyone is doing it, they pose a great enticement to sin. Yet, we should be continually guarding ourselves from these assaults by learning more of God's Word in order to have a solid Biblical foundation to filter out the evils of this world and to avail ourselves to the Spirit's leading.

A Friend of the World is an Enemy of God

James refers to another prohibition of the believer's relations with the world.

> You adulteresses, do you not know that friendship with the world is hostility toward God? Therefore whoever wishes to be a friend of the world makes himself an enemy of God. (James 4:4)

First of all, James is referring to those who are in union with Christ as adulteresses because they have an inordinate affection with the world and its enticements. They are likened to an unfaithful spouse, giving themselves body and soul to another. This symbolism of the unfaithful believer is seen throughout Scripture and was often applied to the nation of Israel in the Old Testament.[2] Dr. Chafer comments:

> This reference to adultery is tied in here with a spiritual usage and therefore means a forsaking of right love and loyalty toward God, substituting in their place the things of this Satan-ruled world.[3]

James then informs these unfaithful believers that their friendship with the world constitutes a hostile relationship with their Heavenly Father. This friendship "involves the adopting of the interests of the world to be one's own."[4] The believer is not to embrace the interests and philosophies of this world system. Instead, he is to become knowledgeable of God's plan and program for his life in order to

---

[2] Cp./w Numbers 25:1; Judges 2:17; Isaiah 1:21; Jeremiah 3:6, 8, 9; Ezekiel 16:32; Hosea 1:2:3

[3] Chafer, 6.180

[4] Zodhiates, G5373

better serve Him. This idea resonates back to a discussion that Jesus had with His disciples:

> No longer do I call you slaves, for the slave does not know what his master is doing; but I have called you friends, for all things that I have heard from My Father I have made known to you (John 15:15).

It is obvious that the more focused the disciples became concerning the Lord's plans, the more intimate their relationship became with Him, and they became a member of His inner circle of friendship rather than that of a slave. We derive from this an exact illustration of the right relationship with our Lord, the true friendship that we are to actively cultivate. It is from this friendship with our Lord that we become partakers of all spiritual blessings (Ephesians 1:3) that are designed to sustain us while we are here in this world.

Are we then to shun all friendships with individuals of the world? This is not the point that James is making – he is not referring to neighborly friendships, but to alliances which compromise Scriptural teachings. To be absolutely clear about this, the believer is **not** to align himself with those whose ideas and philosophies contradict the revealed teachings of the Scriptures. If their ideas and philosophies appear to line up with Scripture, then the believer must determine whether their motives evolve from a sincere desire to glorifying the Lord based on a right interpretation of Scripture.

It is therefore imperative that the believer have a solid foundation of Biblical knowledge to examine the influences of the culture in order to determine how he is to respond. If the believer fails at this point in his Spiritual development, he will permit the reasoning and logic of the world to deceive and sway him from the right relationship with his Lord.

The apostle Paul sums this up in an exceptional manner:

> Therefore as you have received Christ Jesus the Lord, so walk in Him, having been firmly rooted and now being built up in Him and established in your faith, just as you were instructed, and overflowing with gratitude. See

to it that no one takes you captive through philosophy and empty deception, according to the tradition of men, according to the elementary principles of the world, rather than according to Christ (Colossians 2:6-8).

BE NOT CONFORMED TO THE WORLD

Closely associated with the last directive is that the believer ought not to be conformed to this world system. Paul writes:

> Therefore I urge you, brethren, by the mercies of God, to present your bodies a living and holy sacrifice, acceptable to God, which is your spiritual service of worship. And do not be conformed to this world, but be transformed by the renewing of your mind, so that you may prove what the will of God is, that which is good and acceptable and perfect (Romans 12:1-2).

Paul begins with an exhortation for believers to yield themselves to God as a living sacrifice; a sacrifice which is described as being holy (separated from evil and sinfulness) and acceptable or well-pleasing to God. And this, he adds, is your reasonable, or better yet, *rational* service of worship. The readers of this epistle, familiar with the Levitical sacrificial system of the Jewish religion, would recognize the symbolism Paul uses of animal sacrifice. The animal offered had to be without blemish, without any physical deformity. However, after the sacrifice, the animal was dead. Here the sacrifice is to be a living person, themselves. The idea is not profound but obvious – it is to be a moment-by-moment life of sacrifice to the One who has provided the believer with all spiritual blessings for time and eternity.

David Brown's apt summation of this point:

> Such then is the great general duty of the redeemed—*self-consecration*, in our whole spirit and soul and body to Him who hath called us into the fellowship of His Son Jesus Christ. [5] [emphasis his]

[5] Jamieson, R., Fausset, A. R., & Brown, D. (1997) *A Commentary, Critical*

Paul then follows this with an imperative command not to become conformed to this world (lit.: age). The idea here is that believers in their moment-by-moment walk of faith are not to allow the philosophies and affections of this present age to become integrated with the foundational principles of their faith in Christ.

As an example, a humanist may give to the poor because his philosophical thinking motivates him to do something for his fellow man and that this deed along with similar achievements will somehow solve the problems of mankind and bring about a collective paradise with all men living in harmony. The Christian gives to the poor because he wishes to demonstrate the love of Christ to those who are the image-bearers of the Creator, to those who may not have believed in Christ as their Savior. To say that both are doing the same thing only with differing motives is extremely naïve. For those individuals who the humanist has provided for will eventually die, and then what? An eternity separated from God, in the Lake of Fire. However, the Christian's anticipation is that by the witness of his works of love, men will trust in Christ. Although in the end they too will die, the difference is that they will go to an eternal reward – to live forever with their Creator and with all of those who have trusted in Jesus Christ. This is a far better reward than the delusion of a fleeting moment of ecstasy in the humanists' paradise.

So instead of being conformed to this present age, Paul commands that we should "be transformed." The Greek word transform is *metamorphóō,* from which we get our English word metamorphous. Just like the caterpillar changes into a butterfly through the process of metamorphosis, we as believers are to change from our preconceived influences of this world into those who think and act upon the instructions from God's Word. Just as the butterfly is no longer a caterpillar, the believer is no longer the person who embraces worldly viewpoints which conflict with Divine viewpoint.[6]

and Explanatory, on the Old and New Testaments. On spine: Critical and Explanatory Commentary. (Ro 12:2). Oak Harbor, WA: Logos Research Systems, Inc.

[6] "Basic to all the differences between the Christian and the non-Christian views of life is the fact that Christians worship and serve the Creator, while

We are to do this, Paul states, by the renewing of our minds. For this to take place there must be a uprooting of the philosophies and affections of this present age. As Robertson states:

> There must be a radical change in the inner man for one to live rightly in this evil age, "by the renewing of your mind".[7]

The believer must fill his mind with the "mind of Christ" (1 Corinthians 2:16). Not simply asking ourselves in the midst of conflicts: "What Would Jesus Do?" That is what we teach our children as a primer for their Christian walk while they are learning doctrine. Instead, the mature believer ought to *know* what to do in the midst of personal conflict; how to respond in times of political turmoil; where to find comfort in the time of sorrow and grief from losing loved ones. He should be able to resolve ethical dilemmas because of his knowledge of God's viewpoint of the situation. Bishop Trench writes:

> This is the gradual conforming of the man more and more to that new spiritual world into which he has been introduced, and in which he now lives and moves; the restoration of the divine image; and in all this so far from being passive, he must be a fellow-worker with God.[8]

The believer should stand firmly on the principles of God's Word and not allow the world's viewpoint to sway him to think and to do that which would dishonor God and damage his Christian integrity.

The remainder of this verse concludes the divine purpose of the believer's renewal of his mind. It is so that the believer might demonstrate with his life, engaged in the knowledge of Biblical doctrines and empowered by the Holy Spirit, that the will of God is good (devoid of evil or worldly viewpoint), acceptable (because it

---

non-Christians worship and serve the creature," Van Til, Cornelius, (1967) *The Defense of the Faith*, Presbyterian and Reformed Publishing Co., Phillipsburg, NJ, p.31

[7] Robertson, 4.402-403

[8] Trench, pp. 65-66

conforms to the integrity of God), and perfect (i.e. lacking nothing, complete). This is why Paul asserts in 2 Timothy 3:16-17 that:

> All Scripture is inspired by God and profitable for teaching, for reproof, for correction, for training in righteousness; so that the man of God may be adequate, equipped for every good work.

It would be appropriate at this point to note Dr. Kenneth Wuest's conclusion:

> As a result of the Spirit's control of the mental processes of the saint, the latter is enabled to put his life to the test for the purpose of approving it, the specifications being that it conform to the Word of God, and thus, experiencing what obedience is to the Word, and finding out what it feels like to have the Word saturate and control the life, he sees that it really is the Word of God and puts his approval upon it.[9]

LIVE SENSIBLY, RIGHTEOUSLY, AND GODLY IN THE PRESENT AGE

An additional directive from the Apostle Paul concerning our relations with the world and this present age is found in Titus 2:11-12:

> For the grace of God has appeared, bringing salvation to all men, instructing us to deny ungodliness and worldly desires and to live sensibly, righteously and godly in the present age.

In this passage, Paul explains that the teaching of the Word is designed to renew the minds of believers so that they reject the ways of ungodliness and abstain from worldly desires. The tense of the verb "to deny" conveys the determined character of the denial – to break off our engagement in such activities. The idea behind this is

---

[9] Wuest, K. S. (1998) *Wuest's Word Studies from the Greek New Testament,* Vol. 1, Romans (12:2) p. 208, Grand Rapids, MI: Eerdmans

that the believer is to uproot all that is contrary to godliness and the distractions of this world, and to toss them aside as one would weeds from a garden. Just as the weeds will choke and stifle the growth of vegetation, ungodliness and worldly desires will suppress the Spiritual development of the believer in Jesus Christ.

The ultimate purpose of this rejection is so that we might live a manner of life that is pleasing to God. This life is marked, first, by the believer being sensible. To be sensible is to be of sound mind. For the believer to be of sound mind, he must possess the mind of Christ, divine viewpoint. This leads to self-control and self-restraint, which enables the believer to make decisions, not based on emotions, but upon sound Biblical reason.

Secondly, the believer is then able to live righteously. This pertains to our relationship with others. Barnes has a most excellent explanation:

> This refers to the proper performance of our duties to our fellow-men; and it means that religion teaches us to perform those duties with fidelity, according to all our relations in life; to all our promises and contracts; to our fellow-citizens and neighbors; to the poor, and needy, and ignorant, and oppressed; and to all those who are providentially placed in our way who need our kind offices. Justice to them would lead us to act as we would wish that they would towards us.[10]

The third point is that we live a godly life. This relates to a pious life-style pertaining to our relationship with God. It begins with our attitude towards God the Father. Are we truly thankful for the work He has done in our lives? If we are, then we will devote our waking hours in thinking His thoughts, speaking the truth, and doing that which glorifies Him. To think His thoughts we must know His thoughts; this implies that there must be daily study of His Word. To speak the truth, we must have a firm fix on what truth is as defined by His Word. In order to do that which glorifies Him, we must be

---

[10] Barnes, Albert, (2005) *Notes on the New Testament*, Grand Rapids, MI: Baker Books, 12.2.279

mindful of each step we take that we are walking in His will for our lives as defined in His Word.

The characteristics of our Christian life are described here to be (1) inward: a renewed mind that is sensible and sound; (2) outward: an honest and righteous life in the presence of those who we come in contact with every day; (3) God-ward: to live each moment endeavoring to honor and glorify and "love the Lord your God with all your heart, and with all your soul, and with all your mind, and with all your strength" (Mark 12:30).

LIGHTS IN THE WORLD

The reason for living a sensible, righteous and godly life is disclosed by the Apostle Paul in his Epistle to the Philippians:

> Do all things without grumbling or disputing; so that you will prove yourselves to be blameless and innocent, children of God above reproach in the midst of a crooked and perverse generation, among whom you appear as lights in the world (Philippians 2:14-15).

We are to demonstrate by our lives that we are blameless of sin and innocent of evil in order to present an irreproachable testimony while we reside in the midst of this evil culture. Because, as Paul goes on to state, we are to appear (literally: shine) as lights in the world.

Understanding the Biblical imagery of light is imperative to a correct comprehension of the character of God. John wrote:

> This is the message we have heard from Him and announce to you, that God is Light, and in Him there is no darkness at all. (1 John 1:5)

Most students of the Bible assume that the opposite of darkness is light. But this is not the case. Darkness is the absence of light. The terms light and darkness are used metaphorically and relate respectively to righteousness and evil. Since God is light, utterly and completely righteous, there is undeniably no evil (darkness) in Him. He is the perfect One, the Creator of all life and material matter. And since He is absolutely perfect, the violation of His perfect standards must be perpetrated by another agency other than Himself. This is why John was able to make this statement concerning mankind, God's creatures:

> This is the judgment, that the Light has come into the world, and men loved the darkness rather than the Light, for their deeds were evil (John 3:19).

It is the decision of mankind to turn from their righteous Creator and choose to live in the absence of eternal light. It is the reason mankind stands in the need of salvation, and has done so since the final days of Adam and Eve in Eden. It is why God has been determined throughout the ages to shed His light upon all of His creatures, so they might return to Him in eternal fellowship as was His original intent of mankind.

Through the ages, God has provided a means for spreading the light of His provision of salvation to all mankind. In the Old Testament, the nation of Israel was commissioned by Jehovah to be His agent for the dissemination of the Gospel of salvation to the Gentile nations. For God told Abraham:

> In your seed all the nations of the earth shall be blessed, because you have obeyed My voice (Genesis 22:18).[11]

Dr. Clough elaborates further on this:

> Finally God promised exceeding blessing upon this family that would reach outward to all men (Genesis 12:3; 22:18). According to Paul the term "blessing" includes all that is meant by salvation in Christ (Galatians 3:14). The nations, therefore, are blessed "in Abraham" for it is through him that God reaches out to the world. Throughout the rest of the Old Testament the God of Israel is worshipped as the God of all nations (note, for example, the words in Psalm 47:9; 100:1; 126:2b).[12]

---

[11] Note also Genesis 12:3; 18:18

[12] Clough, Charles (2009) "God's Call to Abraham: The Disruptive Truths of Man's Kingdom Rejected." *Part 3: Disruptive Truths of God's Kingdom.* [30

The nation of Israel looked forward to the coming of their Messiah, the light of the world. Their sacrifices were meant to foreshadow the ultimate sacrifice of the Messiah for His people and all the nations. The prophet Isaiah wrote of the future Messiah as the light, whose salvation would reach the ends of the earth.

> I am the Lord, I have called You in righteousness, I will also hold You by the hand and watch over You, And I will appoint You as a covenant to the people, As a light to the nations (Isaiah 42:6).

And,

> I will also make You a light of the nations so that My salvation may reach to the end of the earth (Isaiah 49:6b).

This theme was echoed by Simeon, when Mary and Joseph presented the child Jesus to the Lord in the temple:

> For my eyes have seen Your salvation,
> Which You have prepared in the presence of all peoples,
> A Light of revelation to the Gentiles,
> And the glory of Your people Israel (Luke 2:30-32).

And while the Lord Jesus was on earth, He boldly proclaimed:

> I am the Light of the world; he who follows Me will not walk in the darkness, but will have the Light of life (John 8:12).

Jesus Christ, the Messiah, the light of the world, is the light that came to shine salvation into the darkness of this world system saturated by the evil of Satan and perpetuated by the wickedness of mankind.

And now in this age, the believer as a member of the Church, the body of Christ is commanded by the Apostle Paul:

> Therefore do not be partakers with them; for you were formerly darkness, but now you are Light in the Lord; walk as children of Light (Ephesians 5:7-8).

This affirmation that we are now light in the Lord is further emphasized by Paul:

> But you, brethren, are not in darkness, that the day would overtake you like a thief; for you are all sons of light and sons of day. We are not of night nor of darkness; so then let us not sleep as others do, but let us be alert and sober (1 Thessalonians 5:4-6).

Paul is clearly pointing out a distinction between *The Light*, Jesus Christ, and the believer, light in the Lord/sons of light. The believer is meant to be the reflection of *The Light*. The believer's life is to reflect the light of Christ to a lost and evil culture. In order for a luminary in the night sky to reflect the light of the sun, the sun's rays of light must shine upon it. So it is with the believer as he lives in the 'rays' of the Light of the Lord Jesus Christ. John makes this point regarding the walk of the believer:

> If we say that we have fellowship with Him and yet walk in the darkness, we lie and do not practice the truth; but if we walk in the Light as He Himself is in the Light, we have fellowship with one another, and the blood of Jesus His Son cleanses us from all sin (1 John 1:6-7).

The light of Christ must completely surround and permeate the believer in order for him to reflect the light of the Gospel of Christ. That is why the Biblical instructions concerning the believer's lifestyle are so practical:

> Do not be bound together with unbelievers; for what partnership have righteousness and lawlessness, or what fellowship has light with darkness? (2 Corinthians 6:14)

Additionally Paul emphasizes:

> Therefore let us lay aside the deeds of darkness and put on the armor of light (Romans 13:12b).

The light of Christ reflected by the believer must emanate from his external actions as well as his internal thoughts. In fact, it is essential that the thought life of the believer be renewed first by the Word of

God in order for his external actions to be conformed to the demand of walking in the light. This is why the Psalmist wrote:

> Your word is a lamp to my feet
> And a light to my path (Psalm 119:105).[13]

He knew the importance of filling his mind with that which would be the basis for holy living. If only believers today in a concerted attitude would emulate the desires to allow the light of His Word to become the illuminating power in their lives, The Light of the world would shine as a blaze of glory before this lost culture.

CONCLUSION

The Bible abounds with commands pertaining to the believer's walk of faith. However, these six Biblical directives are specific concerning the believer's conduct as he lives in this world system controlled by Satan. There is great danger for the believer who misunderstands or ignores these instructions. To become overly affectionate with the world system where it contradicts Scripture will lead the believer off the narrow road that leads to life,[14] hindering his spiritual growth and effectiveness. To disregard the obligation of living a godly life destroys the believer's testimony for Christ before fallen man. We must be thoroughly attentive to the culture around us, for they are growing more intolerant towards Christians who maintain the Biblical foundations of our faith, and they are quick to point out the hypocrisy of those who fail to uphold Biblical principles. So it becomes increasingly essential for believers to submit themselves to a life of obedience to their Lord. Therefore, as Paul has stated:

> Be imitators of God, as beloved children and walk in love,
> just as Christ also loved you and gave Himself up for us,
> an offering and a sacrifice to God as a fragrant aroma.
> (Ephesians 5:1-2)

---

[13] Note also: Psalm 43:3; Proverbs 6:23
[14] Matthew 7:14

CHAPTER CHECK

1. Do we have the same world pressures as the 1st Century believers? Name some.

2. What would be a Biblical example of a Christian's love of the world?

3. How does the study of the Word help to keep one unstained by the world?

4. Does avoiding friendship with the world mean that you should not befriend your unsaved neighbors?

5. In what ways can a Christian become conformed to the world?

6. What does it mean to "deny ungodliness"?

7. Describe the difference between light and darkness in the Biblical sense.

PART II:

THE RETURN TO THE FOUNDATIONS

It has been said that the greatest virtue in the Christian life is the knowledge of Bible doctrine. Therefore, a Christian without the basic knowledge of Bible doctrine has little or nothing in his soul that the Holy Spirit can use to energize him to live a spiritually productive and holy life.

The objective of Part II is to explain the foundational principles of the Christian faith. What follows is a brief summary of the truths which are the basics of Christian Orthodoxy.[1] However, they are not meant to be comprehensive in their scope. The student of the Bible should seek further study, availing himself of the bibliography provided. The truths presented here are based upon a correct interpretation of Scripture and have been the established foundations of the Christian faith since the early days of the Church. The church in the 21st Century should therefore aspire to become unified in orthodox doctrine in order to present a united and powerful witness to the world.

---

[1] "Orthodoxy" means a position that conforms to established doctrine.

⊷ 4 ⊶

THE ACCURACY OF TRUTH: SCRIPTURE

The Biblical directives as outlined in the previous chapter, underline the importance of a consistent walk of faith by all individual believers. The prevailing notion that only the pastor, the elders, the deacons and a select few are expected to demonstrate a lifestyle consistent with Biblical teaching has been a detriment to the witness of Christ before the world. The equally baseless opinion by church leaders that the man in the pew is merely a layman and is unable to discern 'deep' Biblical truth has led to a generation of Christians that are unable to fully understand Bible doctrine and to fully exploit its empowering resources for their lives.

In order for the Church of Jesus Christ to become a unified witness for Christ it is essential that all believers adhere to the same foundational principles of the faith. This indicates that primarily *all* believers need to regard God's written Word as wholly accurate and authoritative for their lives and the practice of their faith. The bond that should hold all believers together ought to be that of a cohesive understanding of the revelation that God has given to us concerning Himself and His creation. From His Word we learn all that He desires for us to know concerning His holy character and His righteous demands for His creatures. However, His revelation was not meant to be treated in a relativistic manner. For this approach has already led to instability and confusion within the Church, local and universal. And since God is not a God of confusion,[1] we must strive to become unified in our understanding and application of His revelation.

This chapter pertaining to the Scriptures will entail the study of inspiration, infallibility, inerrancy, interpretation and the methods of teaching.

INSPIRATION

To begin with, there is the question of the authorship of the Bible. Exactly who wrote the Bible? Some might answer that the human authors wrote freely of their own accord or on an impulse. And yet this is not what Scripture suggests as Dr. Bromiley writes:

> Primary here is the divine authorship of Scripture. This is a doctrine plainly taught by Scripture, and neither arbitrarily imported into it nor fancifully extracted from it. Scripture understands itself, not as an essay in human religion but as divine self-revelation.[2]

Scripture clearly establishes its Divine authorship – the Holy Spirit using men to pen the books of the Bible in order to provide a revelation of God to mankind.

A good place to start is to refer to the definition of inspiration as given by Dr. Chafer:

> The theological use of the term *inspiration* is a reference to that controlling influence which God exerted over the human authors by whom the Old and New Testaments were written. It has to do with the reception of the divine message and the accuracy with which it is transcribed [emphasis his].[3]

---

[1] "For God is not a God of confusion but of peace, as in all the churches of the saints" (1 Corinthians 14:33).

[2] Bromiley, Geoffrey W., (1979) "The Interpretation of the Bible," *The Expositor's Bible Commentary,* Grand Rapids, MI: Zondervan, 1.77

[3] Chafer, 1.61

The involvement of God in conveying His Word, as described in this definition, is evidence of His desire to provide men with a revelation of Himself that would be a reliable and coherent foundation for our faith. Therefore, the study of the inspiration of Scripture has as its objective to discern *exactly how* God communicated His Word to the writers of the Bible.

If God's revelation is to be a unifying dynamic for all believers,[4] than there must be certainty that the Bible is an accurate communication from God. The Scripture claims to be inspired by God, and that it contains intrinsic power for the believer:

> All Scripture is inspired by God and profitable for teaching, for reproof, for correction, for training in righteousness; so that the man of God may be adequate, equipped for every good work. (2 Timothy 3:16-17)

The question then is: How did God accomplish this awesome task of communicating His thoughts and ideas to the writers of the books of the Bible? The Greek word translated *inspired* [θεόπνευστος/ *theopneustos*] literally means "God-breathed." God spoke in and through these men. However, there is no Scriptural evidence to indicate that He dictated to them as if they were His secretaries. He conveyed his thoughts to these men by the Holy Spirit, using their intellect, their vocabulary and their personalities to write down His revelation to mankind. As Peter states:

> For no prophecy was ever made by an act of human will, but men moved by the Holy Spirit spoke from God. (2 Peter 1:21)

David likewise stated that his writings originated by the Holy Spirit:

> Now these are the last words of David.
> David the son of Jesse declares,
> The man who was raised on high declares,

---

4 Ephesians 4:5 - "faith" (πίστις) has a lexical definition of: "That which is believed, body of faith or belief, doctrine," see, Arndt, W., Gingrich, F. W., p. 664 §3.

> The anointed of the God of Jacob,
> And the sweet psalmist of Israel,
> The Spirit of the Lord spoke by me,
> And His word was on my tongue. (2 Samuel 23:1-2)

These men wrote only what the divine author intended to reveal to mankind. This means that since we may not have an *exhaustive* revelation of God, we do have *sufficient* revelation for our understanding of His authority over all of His creation. And we may conclude from 2 Timothy 3:16-17, we also have an adequate basis for teaching and training in righteousness.

The fundamental teaching of inspiration, found in most systematic theology textbooks, characterizes it as *verbal, plenary inspiration.* By verbal inspiration it is meant that the Spirit guided the human authors in the choice of their words. The Spirit allowed the writer to use his own vocabulary to express divine truth. By this we are able to obtain an insight into their personality and well as the extent of their knowledge.

Dr. Chafer defines plenary inspiration:

> By *plenary* inspiration is meant that the accuracy which verbal inspiration secures is extended to every portion of the Bible so that it is in all its parts both *infallible* as to truth and *final* as to divine authority [emphasis his].[5]

We are therefore assured of an accurate transmission of the thoughts and ideas which God chose to reveal to man concerning His character and that which pertains to the relationship which He intended with His creatures.

INFALLIBILITY

The Scripture also claims to be infallible, that is, dependable and unfailing as it relates to truth. Regarding this truth, Jesus stated with conviction that "The Scripture cannot be broken"[6] and "Your

---

5 Chafer, 1.71
6 John 10:35

Word is truth."[7] The fact of the matter is that the Bible contains truth from God for all mankind and truth that is accurate, universal in its application, and unable to be negated by any human device or methodology. God substantiates this in Isaiah:

> So will My word be which goes forth from My mouth;
> It will not return to Me empty,
> Without accomplishing what I desire,
> And without succeeding in the matter for which I sent it.
> (Isaiah 55:11)

Peter corroborates:

> So we have the prophetic word made more sure, to which you do well to pay attention as to a lamp shining in a dark place. (2 Peter 1:19a)

If the Word is a dispenser of dependable truth then it stands to reason that we as believers have an immense source of power at our disposal to fulfill the purpose which God has for us and to glorify Him in the midst of a lost generation.

INERRANCY

Closely related to infallibility is the subject of inerrancy which maintains that the Bible is entirely free from errors in its transmission from God to the human authors and then to the manuscripts that they were written upon. An apt definition of inerrancy is given in *The Fundamentals for the Twenty-First Century*:

> Simply put, *inerrancy* means that Scripture in the original manuscripts (*autographs*) does not affirm anything that is contrary to fact, that the Bible *always* speaks the truth concerning *everything* it addresses [emphasis his].[8]

---

[7] John 17:17
[8] Foos Harold D. and Patterson, L. Paige, (2000) "The Revelation, Inspiration, and Inerrancy of the Bible," *The Fundamentals for the Twenty-First Century*, Grand Rapids, MI: Kregel, p. 97

We again refer to the Apostle Peter for further evidence as stated in Scripture:

> So we have the prophetic word made more sure, to which you do well to pay attention as to a lamp shining in a dark place. (2 Peter 1:19a)

The phrase "the prophetic word made more sure" could easily be rendered, as Marvin Vincent does: a surer confirmation of God's truth.[9] The idea according to the lexical definition of the word "sure" is "*reliable, dependable, certain.*" So we are assured that "*we possess the prophetic word as something altogether reliable.*"[10]

The common assumption of unbelievers as well as of some Christians is that there are contradictions in the Bible and therefore it contains errors. This comes from a misunderstanding of the doctrine. It should be noted that inerrancy applies *exclusively* to the original manuscripts of the Old and New Testaments. Geisler points this out:

> If God cannot err, and the original text was breathed out by God, then it follows that the original text of the Bible is without error. Hence, any real errors found in biblical manuscripts or in translations of them were not in the original. Copies of the original are only inspired insofar as they are accurate copies of the original.[11]

Unfortunately, the original manuscripts that the Biblical writers used are not extant today. The modern translations which we use today were derived from copies "which have been in minor detail subjected to scribal errors."[12] However, the science of textual criticism has made great progress in assembling ancient manuscripts and determining, based on objective linguistic measures, what scribal errors have been

---

[9] Vincent, Marvin R. (n/d) *Word Studies in the New Testament*, Peabody, MA: Hendrickson, 1.687

[10] Arndt, W., Gingrich, F. W., p. 137.

[11] Geisler, Norman L., (2002) *Systematic Theology*, Minneapolis, MN: Bethany House, 1.240

[12] Geisler, Norman L., (2003) *Christian Apologetics*, Peabody, MA: Prince Press, p. 363

made in order to reduce the transmission of human error into our modern translations. They endeavor to determine: "What is the original text of the passage?"[13]

Laying aside the matter of what may seem to be contradictions, the main assertion of the doctrine of inerrancy is the veracity of the Bible in all that it proclaims doctrinally or historically. The argument is strengthened by Jesus' statement that "Your Word is truth."[14] Anything that is not truth cannot logically be considered absolute truth. Jesus told the Samaritan woman in John 4:23,

> But an hour is coming, and now is, when the true worshipers will worship the Father in spirit and truth.

It follows then that He would provide for us His standard of truth. Christianity does not claim that the Bible is absolute truth simply because it needs something to back up a preconceived idea – the internal witness of the Bible declares that it is truth. God has therefore provided us with a foundation for determining what truth is according to His standard of holiness. Otherwise, we would be as ships without rudders, drifting in a sea of relativity.

INTERPRETATION

The science of Biblical interpretation is known as hermeneutics. Biblical Hermeneutics provides the believer with the necessary tools for an accurate study and understanding of the Word of God. Paul admonished Timothy concerning just this matter:

> Be diligent to present yourself approved to God as a workman who does not need to be ashamed, accurately handling the word of truth. (2 Timothy 2:15)

Sometimes believers miss the thrust of this verse. Certainly we are exhorted to accurately handle the Word, but it is for the purpose of presenting ourselves approved before God. That is, as we appear

---

[13] Metzger, Bruce M., (2001) *A Textual Commentary on the Greek New Testament*, Stuttgart: United Bible Societies, p. 1

[14] John 17:17

before God in harmony with His standards, we then will stand before mankind as examples of Godliness. If all believers are to stand approved before God as a consolidated front against the evil of this age, then it follows that the criterion by which we live must coincide to His *exact* standard. In order to obtain a unified base for believers there needs to be a singular method of interpreting God's Word. Anything else results in the confusion within Christianity as we see today. Compare this to an army of soldiers who are given battle orders and each soldier understood the orders from different viewpoints. The battle would be lost before it started simply because of the disunity of the combatants. And once they were on the field of battle, there would be no unified battle plan in order to effectively defeat the enemy.

So it is important in this day and age for believers everywhere to have a unified base of understanding God's Word. For without it believers will be in disarray as they step out onto the battlefield of this evil world. Believers need a unified front if they are to present an uncompromising witness to a lost culture.

There are numerous methods of Biblical Interpretation: allegorical, spiritualizing, typological, prophetic, devotional, and rationalistic, to name just a few.[15] However, it is not unreasonable to believe that since God has provided a written revelation concerning Himself, His creation, and His righteous demands for His creatures, that He would provide one which could be easily understood by *all*. This is corroborated by Scripture when Paul wrote:

> For this reason I bow my knees before the Father, from whom every family in heaven and on earth derives its name, that He would grant you, according to the riches of His glory, to be strengthened with power through His Spirit in the inner man, so that Christ may dwell in your hearts through faith; and that you, being rooted and

---

[15] For a complete reading of these and other methods see: McLean, John A., (2000) "The Importance of Hermeneutics," *The Fundamentals for the Twenty-First Century,* Grand Rapids, MI: Kregel, pp. 80-83; Ramm, Bernard, (1956) *Protestant Biblical Interpretation,* Boston, MA: W.A.Wilde, pp. 23-84

grounded in love, *may be able to comprehend with all the saints* what is the breadth and length and height and depth, and to know the love of Christ which surpasses knowledge, that you may be filled up to all the fullness of God [emphasis added].(Ephesians 3:14-19)

Let us therefore examine what is known as the literal or grammatical-historical method of interpretation. Dr. Pentecost provides this definition:

The literal method of interpretation is that method that gives to each word the same exact basic meaning it would have in normal, ordinary, customary usage, whether employed in writing, speaking or thinking.[16]

Pentecost goes on to explain that the words: must retain their normal significance; the historical setting at the time of writing must be considered; the understanding of the grammar and syntax of the original languages should be adhered to; and, the interpretation of figurative language should maintain their literal meanings in spite of the use of symbolic language.[17]

Also of great consideration should be that of the correct interpretation of the context of any given passage. Ramm explains "that a *thought* expressed in a sentence can only be properly deduced when that *thought* is set in the light of the thoughts which precede it and which follow after it [emphasis his]."[18] And in a wider sense, the understanding of any given passage should not contradict the message of the book in which it is written as well as with the entire Bible. The student of the Bible must compare Scripture with Scripture in order to arrive at the proper understanding of God's Word.

From this approach, every believer could be, as it were, on the same page – in agreement of the understanding and application of God's Word. Having the same discernment of God's Word would ensure a basis for absolute truth and a united witness of believers

---

[16] Pentecost, J. Dwight, (1964) *Things to Come*, Grand Rapids, MI: Zondervan, p. 9

[17] Pentecost, pp. 34-44

[18] Ramm, p. 136

would be inescapably observed by the culture at large. For when the Bible commands: "You shall not steal,"[19] there is nothing to read in-between the lines. It clearly means that if something belongs to another, you are not to take it. Or, "Walk by the Spirit, and you will not carry out the desire of the flesh,"[20] plainly means that when the believer is under the controlling influence of the Holy Spirit he will be able to live a life free from carnality. This carnality is further defined by the context of the passage:

> Now the deeds of the flesh are evident, which are: immorality, impurity, sensuality, idolatry, sorcery, enmities, strife, jealousy, outbursts of anger, disputes, dissensions, factions, envying, drunkenness, carousing, and things like these. (Galatians 5:19-21a)

From this list the believer may determine if his life is in alignment with these or with the fruit of the Spirit:

> But the fruit of the Spirit is love, joy, peace, patience, kindness, goodness, faithfulness, gentleness, self-control; against such things there is no law. (Galatians 5:22-23)

Again, there is no hidden meaning or esoteric messages that may be understood differently by different believers.

The chief advantage of the literal method is outlined by Bernard Ramm:

> It seeks to ground interpretations in *facts*. It seeks to rest its case in any given passage on such objective considerations as grammar, logic, etymology, history, geography, archeology or theology [emphasis his].[21]

Additional advantages are explained by Pentecost:

> It gives us a basic authority by which interpretation may be tested. The allegorical method, which depends on the rationalistic approach of the interpreter, or conformity to

---

[19] Exodus 20:15
[20] Galatians 5:16
[21] Ramm, pp. 103-104

a predetermined theological system, leaves one without a basic authoritative test. In the literal method Scripture may be compared with Scripture, which, as the inspired Word of God, is authoritative and the standard by which all truth is to be tested. Related to this we may observe that it delivers us from both reason and mysticism as requisites to interpretation. One does not have to depend upon intellectual training or abilities, nor upon the development of mystical perception, but rather upon the understanding of what is written in its generally accepted sense. Only on such a basis can the average individual understand or interpret the Scriptures for himself.[22]

It cannot be helped but to reiterate that the overall advantage of a unified method of Biblical interpretation employed by the Church of Jesus Christ is that of a consistent witness of the truth of the existence of God and His power to reconcile sinners to Himself.

METHODOLOGY OF TEACHING GOD'S WORD

One of the great misconceptions of Christianity today concerns the character and scope of the pulpit ministry of the local church. There are many who believe the pastor should be physically dynamic in his approach, or one who uses lots of visual aids. On the other hand, there are many who disapprove of the use of visual aids in the Sunday service. There are those who desire that the pastor preach fire and brimstone messages on Sunday morning for the benefit of the unsaved, while others want him to utilize the sermon style consisting of three points and a witty poem. Churches have split or closed up or worse, have maintained a simmering internal hostility over these types of issues. With these divisions over the teaching of God's Word it is no wonder why there are so many doctrinal differences within the Church of Jesus Christ. For whenever Scripture is misinterpreted, there will always be divisions and strife. That is why it is essential for men who have devoted their lives to the teaching of God's Word, and

---

[22] Pentecost, pp. 11-12

the seminaries that train these men,[23] to return to the foundational principles of doctrine. The emphasis should be placed upon the content of the message instead of the style and methods of teaching. Likewise, the recipients of the teaching of God's Word should focus on the content of the message regardless of the individual style and methods of the pastor.[24]

The Objective

To begin with, the Apostle Paul explains the office and objective of the pastor of the local church:

> And He gave some as apostles, and some as prophets, and some as evangelists, and some as pastors and teachers, for the equipping of the saints for the work of service, to the building up of the body of Christ. (Ephesians 4:11-12)

These verses deal with the administrative gifts of the Church. Specific to the present study, the office of the pastor and teacher is shown to be one and the same. This is explained by the unique grammatical construction in the Greek.[25] The man who occupies the pulpit of the local church is to be a pastor – one who has spiritual control over the flock similar to that of a shepherd of a flock of sheep. But he is also

---

[23] Chafer writes: "Indeed, the gifted men must themselves be trained for their tasks and, under modern arrangements, such training is supposed to be provided by the theological seminary." Chafer, Lewis Sperry (1991) *The Epistle to the Ephesians*, Grand Rapids, MI: Kregel, p. 117

[24] "Doctrine must always precede exhortation since in doctrine the saint is shown his exalted position which makes the exhortation to a holy life, a reasonable one, and in doctrine, the saint is informed as to the resources of grace he possesses with which to obey the exhortations." Wuest, K. S. (1998). *Wuest's Word Studies from the Greek New Testament*, Grand Rapids, MI: Eerdmans, Vol. I, "Romans," p 204

[25] "The words 'pastors' and 'teachers' are in a construction called Granville Sharp's rule which indicates that they refer to one individual." Wuest, K. S. (1998). *Wuest's Word Studies from the Greek New Testament*, Grand Rapids, MI: Eerdmans, Vol. I, "Ephesians and Colossians," *p. 101*. See also: Wallace, D. B. (1996). *Greek Grammar Beyond the Basics: An Exegetical Syntax of the Greek New Testament*, Grand Rapids, MI: Zondervan Publishing House, p. 284

to be a teacher – one who instructs the flock in the doctrines of the Word of God. He has the awesome task of edifying believers so that they are equipped for the "work of service." The believer is not to sit around and let the pastor or a few others do the work of service, they are to be actively doing the work of the service. To name a few examples, this could entail visiting the sick, helping those in need of the necessities of life, sharing the Gospel, and prayer.

The secondary purpose given is for the building up of the body of Christ. The word building is the same as construction. If a contractor were to construct a building, he would endeavor to ensure that the building would be solid and able to fulfill the purpose of its design. The pastor-teacher is to be of the same mind. His teaching should enable the members of his church to become able workers because of the substance of that which they are constructed with – sound doctrine.

Dr. Chafer comments:

> Thus it is ordained of God that the greatest service is to be wrought by the saints; but it is also recognized that the saints are to be specifically trained for their task.[26]

Paul goes on in the next verse to explain the ultimate objective for the equipping and building up of the saints:

> Until we all attain to the unity of the faith, and of the knowledge of the Son of God, to a mature man, to the measure of the stature which belongs to the fullness of Christ. (Ephesians 4:13)

Paul understood the necessity of believers achieving and maintaining the unity of the faith.[27] And without this unifying base, believers would not have sufficient knowledge of Jesus Christ nor would they reach their spiritual growth potential. That is why he points out that there is a gauge to evaluate our growth – the fullness of Christ.

Dr. Wuest comments:

---

[26] Chafer, Lewis Sperry (1991) *The Epistle to the Ephesians*, Grand Rapids, MI: Kregel, p. 116
[27] See note 4 above

The expression "the fullness of Christ," refers to the sum of the qualities which make Christ what He is. These are to be imaged in the Church, and when these are in us we shall have reached our maturity and attained to the goal set before us.[28]

From these three verses, Paul illustrates the vital importance of a unified communication of sound doctrine throughout the Church of Jesus Christ. A.T. Robertson stated that "no pastor has finished his work when the sheep fall so far short of the goal."[29] This expresses the tremendous task of the pastor-teacher to feed his flock so that they will achieve the "goal set before us."

The Directive

We can easily see why the Apostle Paul in the early days of the Church stressed the importance of communicating the Word of God to those whom he had instructed in the ministry of pastoral care. To young Timothy he wrote:

I solemnly charge you in the presence of God and of Christ Jesus, who is to judge the living and the dead, and by His appearing and His kingdom: preach the word; be ready in season and out of season; reprove, rebuke, exhort, with great patience and instruction. (2 Timothy 4:1-2)

Paul commanded Timothy to preach the word. The word "preach" simply means to "preach, to herald, proclaim...announce publicly."[30]

Dr. Wuest notes:

The English word "preach" brings to our mind at once the picture of the ordained clergyman standing in his pulpit on the Lord's Day ministering the Word. But the Greek word here (*kērussō*) left quite a different impression with Timothy. At once it called to his mind the Imperial Herald, spokesman of the Emperor, proclaiming in a

---

[28] Wuest, Vol. 1, "Ephesians and Colossians," p. 102
[29] Robertson, 4.538
[30] Zodhiates, G2784

formal, grave, and authoritative manner which must be listened to, the message which the Emperor gave him to announce. It brought before him the picture of the town official who would make a proclamation in a public gathering. The word is in a construction which makes it a summary command to be obeyed at once. It is a sharp command as in military language. This should be the pattern for the preacher today. His preaching should be characterized by that dignity which comes from the consciousness of the fact that he is an official herald of the King of kings. It should be accompanied by that note of authority which will command the respect, careful attention, and proper reaction of the listeners. [31]

Paul admonishes Timothy to be ready at any time to preach and then defines the scope of his preaching by way of three commands: to reprove, which means to explain error from a Scriptural perspective; to rebuke, meaning to "warn in order to prevent an action"[32] that may lead to sin; to exhort, meaning to appeal to his listeners to be obedient to the Word and to avoid temptation and sin. Paul then explains to Timothy that he should preach with *great* patience towards his listeners. The idea is that he should exhibit a genuine understanding that some may not readily follow his directives and so he must be patient with them and not frustrate them by being overbearing. And regardless of any of their shortcomings, Paul encourages Timothy to be persistent in instructing them in the doctrines of the faith.

This demonstrates Paul's emphasis that he placed on comprehensive teaching. Paul firmly believed that the Christian's life should characterize Christ and that it could be accomplished only through the knowledge and implementation of doctrine.[33] The same emphasis of teaching God's Word should be advocated in the church of the 21st

---

[31] Wuest, Vol. II, "Pastoral Epistles," p.154
[32] Arndt, W., Gingrich, F. W., p. 303
[33] Romans 15:14; 1 Corinthians 1:5; 2 Corinthians 2:14, 6:1-10, 8:7-9; Ephesians 1:17, 3:19, 4:13; Philippians 3:8; Colossians 1:5-6

Century. Instead the pulpit is used many times as a means to preach social change, personal opinions and politically correct values.

Merrill Unger states what is true preaching:

> True preaching, although it involves teaching, goes beyond it (teaching), enforcing with unction and power the claims of the Word of God upon the needs of the hearers...There can be no substitute for the authoritative declaration of the Word and will of God directed toward meeting human needs by the Spirit-chosen and Spirit-anointed man of God.[34]

Expository Preaching

Dr. Unger's book, *Principles of Expository Preaching*, originally published in 1955, explores what has now become a lost method of preaching God's Word – expository preaching. He characterizes this method as a systematic presentation of the Word that is Bible-centered, appealing to the emotion and the will, and one that treats the Scriptures as a "coherent and coordinated body of revealed truth."[35] It is the same approach which the apostles used during the early days of the Church. They continually presented Scripture as the revealed Word of God and consistently appealed to the emotion and will of those with whom they spoke.

Dr. Unger goes on to point out that the expositor must be adequately equipped for the preaching of the Word. He should have a broad education which includes history, psychology, sociology, as well as a thorough knowledge of systematic theology (the foundations for our faith) and of the original languages, Hebrew and Greek. The importance of knowing the original languages cannot be minimized. When a document is being translated into another language, there are many grammatical, syntactical and vocabulary problems to be considered.

---

[34] Unger, Merrill F. (1977) *Principles of Expository Preaching*, Grand Rapids, MI: Zondervan, pp.12-13

[35] Unger, pp. 33-36

Dr. Unger notes that:

> Without a knowledge of the original languages an expositor is entirely dependent upon secondary sources for his knowledge of what the Scriptures teach. This is the case inasmuch as only the original is the primary source. To the extent that the expositor is ignorant of the meaning of the original, he is denied access to the final court of appeal and the authoritative and trustworthy decision it is able to render.[36]

The interpretation of God's Word is never based upon what *feels* or *seems* to be the meaning as viewed by one person or one denomination; but a careful and systematic analysis of the original texts will reveal the true significance of God's Word. Also, referring to the original languages of the Bible as the "final court of appeal"[37] will shed light on the difficult passages of God's revelation.

The methodology of the pulpit ministry, therefore, requires a man with the gift of pastor-teacher, who is adequately skilled in the study of the Word of God and is Biblically faithful in the dissemination of these truths to the members of his flock. His objective is to encourage his flock to become knowledgeable in the Word in order for them to reach their spiritual growth potential and to execute the plan that God has for their lives, moment-by-moment glorifying Him.

CONCLUSION

The aim of this chapter was to solidify the basis for the Christian's belief in the Bible as the authoritative revelation from God. That which would provide sufficient knowledge of his Creator, the plan He has for the salvation of mankind, and the directives for living a life through the power of the Holy Spirit. Since God has provided this to all believers for the same purpose, then it follows that in order to avoid confusion within the universal body of believers, their understanding of His revelation ought to be the same.

---

[36] Unger, p. 70
[37] Unger, p. 70

The centrality of the Christian faith rests solely upon the person and work of Jesus Christ. Likewise, our knowledge of Him is centrally located in His written revelation: Scripture. The Scriptures claim internally to be inspired by the Holy Spirit, infallible in its presentation of truth and free from human errors in its transmission. If Christianity were to disregard this objective truth concerning His revelation, then what would remain would be a religion based on subjective truth – men seeking the approval of God based on their own merits instead of relying upon the grace of God. The shingle over the door of the church might say "Christian", but it would be destitute of absolute truth and the power of the Holy Spirit.

Unfortunately, this is what has occurred in many churches today across the United States. It brings to mind something cleverly written (in a biblical-type font, no less!) on the back cover of the 1971 Jethro Tull *Aqualung* album:

> In the beginning Man created God; and in the image of Man created he him.
>
> And Man gave unto God a multitude of names, that he might be Lord over all the earth when it was suited to Man.
>
> And on the seven millionth day Man rested and did lean heavily on his God and saw that it was good…
>
> And Man became the God he had created and with his miracles did rule over all the earth.
>
> But as all these things did come to pass, the spirit that did cause man to create his God lived on within all men…[38]

It is a tragedy that many Christian churches as well as many religions have done just this: created a god in their own image, and they now rest upon the laurels of their works, their human activities without the power of the Holy Spirit. The Bible warns that these works are purely wood, hay, and stubble – worthless and of no value in God's sight.[39]

---

[38] Jethro Tull, *Aqualung*, Chrysalis Records CDR1044, 1971
[39] 1 Corinthians 3:10-14

There is a vital need to return to the foundational principles of the Christian faith that are contained in His authoritative Word, with its proper interpretation and exposition, in order to fully realize His power in our lives to become a unified witness to a lost culture. Without a unified witness to confront the spiritual problems of our culture, the world will view us as a dysfunctional and abnormal segment of society.

CHAPTER CHECK

1. How did God communicate His written Word?

2. Explain infallibility and inerrancy.

3. What is the system of Bible interpretation?

4. Name and explain the various systems of interpretation.

5. What is expository teaching?

6. How important is the knowledge of the original languages for the teaching of God's Word?

7. Why do we believe the Bible to be an authoritative revelation from God?

ᎦᏛ 5 ᏆᏉ

THE DOCTRINE OF GOD

DOES GOD EXIST?

The existence of God cannot be proven by any methodology of man (i.e. science, philosophy, mathematics). The presupposition of the existence of God is based solely on the fact that God has stated in His Word that He exists.[1] The belief of His existence becomes a matter of faith for the individual. For man to state that God does not exist does not negate the fact of His existence. In other words, God doesn't cease to exist because the atheist says He doesn't exist. Neither does He exist for the Christian in order to relieve an emotional or psychological need; He exists because He says that He does in His self-revealing Scriptures. The purpose of revealing Himself to His creatures is so they might be reconciled to Him and to enjoy a personal relationship with Him.

CAN MAN KNOW GOD?

The answer to this question is contained in the revelation which He has given to us: the Bible. It is from this revelation that He

---

[1] Genesis 1:1 states that God was in the beginning, without any argumentation of His existence. Later, He revealed Himself to Moses by stating: "I AM WHO I AM" (Exodus 3:14), referring to His self-existence.

has provided man with reliable information to know Him. Unger points out:

> Perfect or complete knowledge of God is not attainable by man upon the earth. But equally true is that the Scriptures represent God as revealing Himself to man and that a sufficient though limited measure of true knowledge of God is put within the reach of human beings. The important distinction to be maintained at this point is that between partial and perfect knowledge.[2]

Therefore, the Bible does not provide an *exhaustive* knowledge of Him. But what it does supply is *sufficient* for us to know of Him and His plan for our lives.[3] There is no other means by which we are able to learn of Him, but by that which has been revealed in His Word. Dr. Chafer writes:

> Turning to the Scriptures, it will be observed immediately that God is not specifically defined in any one assertion, but His existence and attributes are assumed and do appear only as the text in various places and in manifold terms sets forth what He is and what He does.[4]

By the study of His Word, the believer can learn the characteristics and essence of God. It is important to note that "God is one Being (essence), but He has many attributes (properties)."[5] Theologians have catalogued these attributes as the Westminster Larger Confession depicts them:

> God is a Spirit, (John 4:24) in and of himself infinite in being, (Exod. 3:14, Job 11:7–9) glory, (Acts 7:2) blessedness, (1 Tim. 6:15) and perfection; (Matt. 5:48) all-sufficient, (Gen. 17:1) eternal, (Ps. 90:2) unchangeable, (Mal. 3:6, James 1:17) incomprehensible, (1 Kings 8:27) every where

---

[2] Unger, Merrill F., (1988) *The New Unger's Bible Dictionary*, Chicago, IL: Moody Press, p.481

[3] John 17:3; Romans 1:19-20; Ephesians 1:17; Colossians 1:10; 1 John 5:20

[4] Chafer, 1.188

[5] Geisler, Norman L., (2002) *Systematic Theology*, Minneapolis, MN: Bethany House, 2.19

present, (Ps. 139:1–13) almighty, (Rev. 4:8) knowing all things, (Heb. 4:13, Ps. 147:5) most wise, (Rom. 16:27) most holy, (Isa. 6:3, Rev. 15:4) most just, (Deut. 32:4) most merciful and gracious, long-suffering, and abundant in goodness and truth. (Exod. 34:6)[6]

God is the absolute embodiment of all attributes ascribed to Him. In other words, He is absolutely holy, He has absolute knowledge, and He has absolute power over all of His creation, and so on. It is said that God has "no potential", meaning that there is nothing new for Him to learn since He is all knowing and possesses all knowledge. He is the quintessence of perfection.

THE TRIUNE GOD

The doctrine of the Triune God or the Trinity is a Biblical truth even though the term is never stated in Scripture. Dr. Ryrie summarizes it thus:

> There is only one God, but in unity of the Godhead there are three eternal and coequal Persons, the same in substance but distinct in subsistence. [7]

By *substance* and *subsistence* is meant that all three members are of the same essence (deity) and eternal (always existed), respectively.

The fact that there are three members of the eternal Godhead is confirmed by passages in both the Old and New Testaments. The Hebrew word used of God in the Old Testament is the plural word *Elohim*. This term along with the use of plural pronouns places emphasis upon the plurality of persons within the Godhead (Genesis 1:1, 26). In the New Testament the emphasis upon the plurality of persons within the Godhead is demonstrated by "their separate responsibilities for the purposes of redemption"[8] (Matthew 28:19).

---

[6] *The Westminster Larger Catechism: With scripture proofs.* 1996 (Question 7). Oak Harbor, WA: Logos Research Systems, Inc.

[7] Ryrie, Charles C., (1995) *The Ryrie Study Bible*: Expanded Edition, NASB, Chicago, IL: Moody Press, p. 2058

[8] Chafer, 7.307

The three members of the Godhead are: the Father, the author of the plan of salvation; the Son, Jesus Christ, begotten (however, not made) of the Father, who executes the plan of salvation by his substitutionary death upon the cross; the Holy Spirit, who proceeds from the Father and the Son, who empowers believers to fulfill the purpose for which they have been saved.

CONCLUSION

The truth of the existence of the God of the Bible is a matter of personal faith in Him, based upon the fact that He has revealed Himself to mankind. His self-revelation includes creation, His Word, and His Son, Jesus Christ.

Paul wrote in Romans 1:20:

> For since the creation of the world His invisible attributes, His eternal power and divine nature, have been clearly seen, being understood through what has been made, so that they are without excuse.

Man merely needs to look around and see the handiwork of the Almighty as proof of His existence.

God has also revealed to us sufficient knowledge of Himself in His Word, describing who He is, His design for the ages, and the plan He has for us in time and eternity.

And the most demonstrative revelation of God was the incarnation of His Son, Jesus Christ. This unique person of the universe, the God-man, walked among men, was tempted at all points, yet without sin, and suffered and died for the sins of the world. The writer of Hebrews commented:

> God, after He spoke long ago to the fathers in the prophets in many portions and in many ways, in these last days has spoken to us in His Son, whom He appointed heir of all things, through whom also He made the world.[9]

---

[9] Hebrews 1:1-2

God proclaims in Scripture that He *does* exist and that He has revealed Himself to man so that he might know His awesome character and to have fellowship with Him for all time and eternity. Because He "desires all men to be saved and to come to the knowledge of the truth,"[10] man is now responsible to respond to his Creator in faith in order to enjoy His offer of salvation.

CHAPTER CHECK

1. On what basis do we believe that God exists?

2. Are we able to obtain exhaustive knowledge of God from His Word?

3. Can we learn more about God apart from the Scriptures?

4. What are some of the characteristics of God?

5. How do these characteristics compare with those of man?

6. Explain the triune nature of God.

7. Are there Old Testament proofs of the triune God?

---

[10] 1 Timothy 2:4

❧ 6 ❧

THE DOCTRINE OF JESUS CHRIST

His Deity

The greatest assault on the person of Jesus Christ is that which concerns His deity. This is true today as it has been over the centuries. Believers and unbelievers alike have attempted to disprove and repudiate the fact that Jesus Christ is true deity. Without a Jesus who is deity the Christian faith is devoid of a foundation. However, the true believer does not hold to this tenet of faith simply because he needs a foundational truth to prop up his belief system. The fact lies in the historical truth claims of Jesus recorded in Scripture. He claimed to be deity – declaring His oneness with the Father: "I and the Father are one;"[1] "...that they may all be one; even as You, Father, are in Me and I in You;"[2] and asserting His preexistence: "Truly, truly, I say to you, before Abraham was born, I am."[3]

Not only do we have Jesus' declarations, His apostles made similar pronouncements. Thomas, the one who was cynical concerning the resurrected Christ, stated upon placing his fingers into the nail prints and his hand into Jesus' pierced side: "My Lord and my God!"[4]

---

[1] John 10:30
[2] John 17:21
[3] John 8:58
[4] John 20:28

When Peter was asked by Our Lord, "But who do you say that I am?" Peter answered, "You are the Christ, the Son of the living God."[5]

We also have the witness of the writers of the New Testament regarding His deity: Paul in his epistle to Titus states that believers should be "looking for the blessed hope and the appearing of the glory of our great God and Savior, Christ Jesus"[6]

John attests to His deity and His preexistence at the outset of his Gospel account:

> In the beginning was the Word, and the Word was with God, and the Word was God. He was in the beginning with God. (John 1:1-2)

The writer of the book of Hebrews quotes Psalm 45:6, an Old Testament proof statement of God the Father concerning the deity of His Son, Jesus Christ:

> But of the Son He says, "Your throne, O God, is forever and ever, And the righteous scepter is the scepter of His kingdom. (Hebrews 1:8)

The Father also testified to Jesus' deity while John was baptizing Him. His words were recorded:

> This is My beloved Son, in whom I am well-pleased. (Matthew 3:17)

Those "Christians" who deny the deity of Jesus Christ, want to maintain their faith in Jesus as a good teacher and example of Godliness. They assert that the writers of Scripture collaborated to exaggerate the claims of Jesus' deity. This leads back to the slippery slope of discrediting the truth claims and authority of Scripture.

Christians cannot repudiate the Jesus of the Bible without the foundation of their faith collapsing. To dismiss the Scriptures concerning Jesus Christ is to dismiss the truth claims of Jesus Christ. Without the truth claims which Jesus spoke, one is left with a straw man and blank spaces representing His words in which anyone can

---

5 Matthew 16:16
6 Titus 2:13

place words that agree with their relativistic image of Jesus – a good man, a good teacher. But it is never the same Jesus of history, the one whose person and works are recorded in the authoritative accounts of Scripture.

C. S. Lewis wrote concerning this issue:

> I am trying here to prevent anyone saying the really foolish thing that people often say about Him: "I'm ready to accept Jesus as a great moral teacher, but I don't accept His claim to be God." That is one thing we must not say. A man who was merely a man and said the sort of things Jesus said would not be a great moral teacher. He would either be a lunatic – on a level with the man who says he is a poached egg – or else he would be the Devil of Hell. You must make your choice. Either this man was, and is, the Son of God: or else a madman or something worse. You can shut Him up for a fool, you can spit at Him and kill Him as a demon; or you can fall at His feet and call Him Lord and God. But let us not come with any patronizing nonsense about His being a great human teacher. He has not left that open to us. He did not intend to.[7]

Therefore it can be stated that Jesus Christ is true deity. Scripture further demonstrates that He possesses all the attributes of the Godhead. He is: *eternal* (Micah 5:2); *immutable* (Malachi 3:6; Hebrews 13:8); *omnipotent* (Philippians 3:21; John 2:1-11, and all miracles He performed); *omniscient* (John 4:18; 6:64); *omnipresent* (Ephesians 1:23; Matthew 18:20; 28:20).[8]

His Humanity

What about His humanity? Wasn't Jesus human? How can He be both human and deity? Scripture may not answer these questions exhaustively, but it does so in providing sufficient understanding

---

[7] Lewis, C. S., (2001) *Mere Christianity*, SanFransico, CA: Harper Collins, p. 52

[8] For further study, see Chafer, *Systematic Theology*, 1.340-342

of the most unique person of the universe – the God-man, Jesus Christ.

His birth was predicted by Isaiah (7:14); He has a birth record (Luke 2:1-7); He has a genealogy (Matthew 1:1-17; Luke 3:23-38). He experienced human characteristics: thirst (John 19:28); hunger (Luke 4:2); He was tired (John 4:6); He slept (Mark 4:38); He was tempted (Luke 4:1-13); He wept (John 11:35). Scripture concludes that He was born like all other humans, He lived a life like all other humans, and He was able to die like all other humans (John 19:33).

HIS TWO NATURES

Just like the doctrine of the triune Godhead is never specifically mentioned in Scripture, the truth of the two natures of Jesus Christ is merely presented, but never expounded upon thoroughly. We have demonstrated in the first two sections of this doctrine of Jesus Christ that Scripture establishes the truth concerning the two natures of Jesus Christ – deity and human. This has come to be known in theology as the doctrine of the *hypostatic union*. The term hypostatic is derived from the word hypostasis, which has as its basic meaning: the substance or essential nature of an individual.[9] Dr. Chafer states:

> The expression *hypostatic union* is distinctly theological and is applicable only to Christ in whom, as in no other, two distinct and dissimilar natures are united...that in this union, that which is divine is in no way degraded by its amalgamation with that which is human; and, in the same manner and completeness, that which is human is in no way exalted or aggrandized above that which is unfallen humanity. [emphasis his][10]

The church throughout its early centuries had struggled with this concept. Church councils met to formulate sound doctrine based

---

[9] *Webster's*, p. 410
[10] Chafer, 1.382

upon a correct interpretation of Scripture. This very issue was the subject of a number of councils, beginning with the Nicene Council of 325 A.D. The council at Ephesus in 431 A.D. fixed the orthodox doctrine of the person of Christ.[11] It was then further clarified at the Chalcedon Council of 451 A.D. and Constantinople Council in 553 A.D.:

> For in teaching that the only-begotten Word was united hypostatically [to humanity] we do not mean to say that there was made a mutual confusion of natures, but rather each [nature] remaining what it was, we understand that the Word was united to the flesh. Wherefore there is one Christ, both God and man, consubstantial with the Father as touching his Godhead, and consubstantial with us as touching his manhood.[12]

The 1646 Westminster Confession of Faith was drafted specifically "to bring the Church of England into greater conformity with the Church of Scotland and the Continental Reformed churches."[13] Here is their skillful restatement of this doctrine:

> The Son of God, the second person in the Trinity, being very and eternal God, of one substance and equal with the Father, did, when the fulness of time was come, take upon Him man's nature, (John 1:1,14, 1 John 5:20, Phil. 2:6, Gal. 4:4) with all the essential properties, and common infirmities thereof, yet without sin; (Heb. 2:14,16–17, Heb. 4:15) being conceived by the power of the Holy Ghost, in the womb of the virgin Mary, of her substance. (Luke 1:27,31,35, Gal. 4:4) So that two whole, perfect, and distinct natures, the Godhead and the manhood, were inseparably joined together in one person, without conversion, composition, or confusion. (Luke 1:35, Col.

---

[11] Schaff, Philip, (2006) *History of the Christian Church*, Peabody, MA: Hendrickson, 3.726-727

[12] Schaff, Philip, (1997) *The Nicene and Post-Nicene Fathers, Second Series*, Albany, OR: The Ages Digital Library Collection, 14.605-606

[13] Orthodox Presbyterian Church, "Confession and Catechisms" (2010) www.opc.org/preface.html [31 May, 2011]

2:9, Rom. 9:5, 1 Pet. 3:18, 1 Tim. 3:16) Which person is very God, and very man, yet one Christ, the only Mediator between God and man. (Rom. 1:3–4, 1 Tim. 2:5)[14]

In summary, Charles Clough emphasizes the most important point of hypostatic union is that Christ is:

> "Undiminished deity united with true humanity without confusion in one person forever."[15]

The reason why this is critical to our understanding of this doctrine is thus: Christ existed prior to His incarnation as true deity, so by taking on the nature of humanity, without its fusion with His divine nature, it qualified Him to become the mediator between God and man.

His Mediatorship

For there is one God, and one mediator also between God and men, the man Christ Jesus" 1 Timothy 2:5

Because sin sets man at variance with his Creator, there is a necessity for one to act as a mediator between him and God. Man in his sinful condition cannot represent himself, for the holy God cannot associate with unrighteousness. It necessitates one who can represent mankind in his need of reconciliation with God.

A mediator as defined by Dr. Wuest:

> The word "mediator" is *mesitēs* (μεσίτης), "one who intervenes between two, either in order to make or restore peace and friendship, or to form a compact or ratify a covenant."[16]

In this case, Jesus Christ intervenes to restore peace and friendship

---

[14] *The Westminster Confession of Faith* (1996) Oak Harbor, WA: Logos Research Systems, Inc., Chapter VIII, 2

[15] Clough, Charles (2009) "Lesson 112 - Review Incarnation (OT points to deity of Christ), Hypostatic Union" *Part 5: Confrontation with the King.* [30 May, 2011] http://www.bibleframework.com/bf-notes/Bible-Framework-Part-5.pdf p.49

[16] Wuest, Vol. II, "The Pastoral Epistles," p. 41

between man and his Creator. The mediator must be able to share common ground with each party – deity and humanity. Jesus Christ alone has just the credentials to be the mediator between God and man.

Chafer explains:

> The fact of His two natures is required for such a responsibility. In Him both Deity and humanity do meet, of course, and in Him the full representation of each is secured or perfected. He must be a sinless man on whom no charge rests, first of all, otherwise He needs a mediator Himself. He must be actually God likewise, not a mere agent of representation. Job's "daysman" then is the precise thought – one who has a right to lay His hand on God in behalf of man and to lay His hand on man in behalf of God. This indeed was Job's cry of appeal unto God, according to Job 9:33.[17]

Calvin emphasized how vitally important this is to mankind:

> It deeply concerned us, that he who was to be our Mediator should be very God and very man. If the necessity be inquired into, it was not what is commonly termed simple or absolute, but flowed from the divine decree on which the salvation of man depended.[18]

Scripture supplies the qualifications necessary for this role of mediator. The following discussion draws upon a section from Charles Hodge's *Systematic Theology* concerning these qualifications.[19] First, according to the writer of the epistle to the Hebrews, He is to be a man:

> Therefore, since the children share in flesh and blood, He Himself likewise also partook of the same, that through death He might render powerless him who had the power of death, that is, the devil, and might free those who

[17] Chafer, 7.235
[18] Calvin, J., & Beveridge, H. (2009) *Institutes of the Christian Religion,* Peabody, MA: Hendrickson, p. 297
[19] Hodge, Charles (2001) *Systematic Theology,* Peabody, MA: Hendrickson, 2:456-459

through fear of death were subject to slavery all their lives. For assuredly He does not give help to angels, but He gives help to the descendant of Abraham. Therefore, He had to be made like His brethren in all things, so that He might become a merciful and faithful high priest in things pertaining to God, to make propitiation for the sins of the people. (Hebrews 2:14-17)

The entire passage clearly asserts that this work could not have been accomplished by an angel or another human being, since it is speaking of the Son of God, Jesus Christ (Hebrews 1:8). This same God-man sat down in a place in which He alone is worthy of occupying, at the right hand of the Majesty on high – this indicated that He had concluded His work of salvation for all mankind (Hebrews 1:3).

Secondly, the mediator must be sinless. Christ, in His death on the cross, represented the anti-type of the Old Testament sacrificial system. The animals that were offered were to be a perfect specimen, without any physical defect. Hodge explains:

> Under the law the victim offered on the altar must be without blemish. Christ, who was to offer Himself unto God as a sacrifice for the sins of the world, must be Himself free from sin. The High Priest, therefore, who becomes us, He whom our necessities demand, must be holy, harmless, undefiled, and separate from sinners. (Hebrews 7:26) He was, therefore, "without sin." (Hebrews 4:15; 1 Peter 2:22) [20]

This fulfills the representational analogy which was given to the Jews in Old Testament times of the necessity of a perfect sacrifice in order to absolve one from their sins. Christ, who lived a perfect life, a life in which He experienced the same temptations as we do, was qualified in all points to be the mediator between man and God.

Which brings us to the third qualification – He must be of a divine nature. Hodge develops this idea:

> The blood of no mere creature could take away sin. It was

---

[20] Hodge, 2:457

only because our Lord was possessed of an eternal Spirit that the one offering of Himself has forever perfected them that believe. None but a divine person could destroy the power of Satan and deliver those who were led captive by him at his will. None but He who had life in Himself could be the source of life, spiritual and eternal, to his people. None but an almighty person could control all events to the final consummation of the plan of redemption, and could raise the dead; and infinite wisdom and knowledge are requisite in Him who is to be judge of all men, and the head over all to his Church. None but one in whom dwelt all the fulness of the Godhead could be the object as well as the source of the religious life of all the redeemed. [21]

The blood sacrifice of bulls and goats was never meant to be anything other than a foreshadowing of the One who is qualified to act as man's mediator between him and God (Hebrews 10:4-10). Because of Christ's perfect life as the unique person of the universe and only through the shed blood of His perfect sacrifice could man be eternally reconciled with his Creator (Hebrews 9:11-14).

CONCLUSION

Jesus Christ is the unique person of the universe. He is true God and true man. The evidence of this fact is based upon the authoritative claims of Scripture. As already cited, the apostles believed in His deity. And since Jesus Himself declared to be equal with the Father, there can be no middle ground in believing this truth. He must be taken at His word or be deemed a lunatic.

The fact that Jesus possessed both the nature of God and the nature of man, qualified Him to be a fitting mediator between man and God. And because Jesus lived a holy, sinless life, He was able to satisfy the Father's demand of a spotless sacrifice for the remission of sins.

These are the important issues that the church in the 21st Century

---

[21] Hodge, 2.457

should maintain as universal truths concerning the person and work of Jesus Christ. Without a unified consensus to these truths, we send a mixed and unsavory message to the culture around us.

CHAPTER CHECK

1. How would you explain the fact that Jesus is God?

2. Does Jesus Christ possess attributes of God? Name some.

3. What are some of the Scripture proofs to Christ's humanity?

4. What does *hypostatic union* mean and how does it apply to Jesus Christ?

5. Why does man need Jesus Christ to be his mediator?

6. What are the Biblical qualifications of a mediator?

↬ 7 ↫

THE DOCTRINE OF THE HOLY SPIRIT

It seems reasonable to suggest that the church in the 21st Century should desire a truly Biblical understanding of the person of the Godhead who empowers believers in their daily lives – the Holy Spirit. To slight or trivialize the need for an authoritative and definitive doctrine concerning the Holy Spirit would logically diminish an invaluable power source specifically designated to enlighten and energize believers to fulfill their purpose in serving God. And yet this has been an ever present problem within the church over the centuries.

This section examines His person, His attributes of deity, Old Testament evidence, New Testament evidence, and His works.

His Person

There seems to be much confusion concerning the reality of this person of the Triune Godhead. He is often considered to be merely a feeling to be experienced instead of the real person that He is. Dr. Chafer expounds upon this:

> If actions and revealed characteristics can intimate personality, the Holy Spirit's personality is more sustained

by evidence than that of the Father, since the Spirit is the Executive, the Creator of the universe, the divine Author of the Scriptures, the Generator of Christ's humanity, the Regenerator of those who believe, and the direct source of every factor in a spiritual Christian's life.[1]

The Scriptures unquestionably presents the Holy Spirit as one of the personages of the Triune Godhead. And this has posed opposition within Christianity, as Dr. Chafer comments further:

Naturally those who oppose themselves against the truth that God subsists in three equal Persons have always sought to degrade the Spirit to a mere influence, as they have sought to degrade the Son to a mere man.[2]

Despite these oppositions, the Bible gives ample evidences that the Holy Spirit is indeed a person and an equal member of the Godhead. John expresses in his Gospel account that the Spirit is a person when he uses the masculine pronouns in the original Greek:

When the Helper comes, whom I will send to you from the Father, that is the Spirit of truth who proceeds from the Father, *He* will testify about Me. (John 15:26 [emphasis added])

And:

But when *He*, the Spirit of truth, comes, *He* will guide you into all the truth; for *He* will not speak on *His* own initiative, but whatever *He* hears, *He* will speak; and *He* will disclose to you what is to come. (John 16:13 [emphasis added])

Paul wrote that the Spirit was able to know and understand the deep things of God (1 Corinthians 2:10-11), that He has a will (1 Corinthians 12:11), and that He has feeling and can be grieved (Ephesians 4:30).

---

[1] Chafer, 6.22
[2] Chafer, 1.397-398

HIS ATTRIBUTES OF DEITY

Since the Holy Spirit is God, He possesses the same attributes of deity as the Father and the Son. These attributes of deity are the credentials of the Godhead; credentials that are never perfectly evidenced in any other being.

The following list and appropriate Scripture references serves to substantiate the point.

- *Eternal:* Hebrews 9:14 – How much more will the blood of Christ, who through the eternal Spirit offered Himself without blemish to God, cleanse your conscience from dead works to serve the living God?

- *Omnipresent:* Psalm 139:7 – Where can I go from Your Spirit? Or where can I flee from Your presence? Also, 1 Corinthians 6:19.

- *Omniscient:* 1 Corinthian 2:10 – For to us God revealed them through the Spirit; for the Spirit searches all things, even the depths of God.

- *Omnipotent:* 1 Peter 3:18 – For Christ also suffered once for sins, the just for the unjust, that He might bring us to God, being put to death in the flesh but made alive by the Spirit. [NKJV]

- *Truth:* 1 John 5:6b – It is the Spirit who testifies, because the Spirit is the truth.

- *Holy:* It is the title given Him by the various authors of the New Testament. Matthew 12:32; Mark 12:36; Luke 11:13; John 14:26; Ephesians 1:13, 4:30; Hebrews 2:4; 2 Peter 1:21; Jude 20.

- *Love:* Galatians 5:22 – But the fruit of the Spirit is love…

OLD TESTAMENT EVIDENCE

Much of the examination of the Holy Spirit has thus far relied heavily on New Testament passages. In spite of the fact that the title "Holy Spirit" occurs only 3 times in the Old Testament,[3] it does speak of the Holy Spirit concerning His person and existence. Dr. Hodge comments:

> In the Old Testament, all that is said of Jehovah is said of the Spirit of Jehovah…The expressions, Jehovah said, and, the Spirit said, are constantly interchanged; and the acts of the Spirit are said to be acts of God.[4]

Further evidence explains His working in lives and events of the Old Testament and prior to the establishment of the Church of Jesus Christ:

1. *Creates the universe and man* – Genesis 1:2; Job 33:4.

2. *Equipped individuals for service* – Judges 3:10; 14:6

3. *Inspired the prophets* – Acts 28:25-26; 2 Peter 1:21

4. *Inspiration of Scriptures* – 2 Timothy 3:16

5. *Produced moral living* – Psalm 143:10; Nehemiah 9:20

6. *Foretold the coming of the Messiah* – Isaiah 9:2-7; 42:1-4

7. *The incarnation of Jesus Christ* – Luke 1:35

The fact that the Holy Spirit is not simply a New Testament figure is clearly seen by the above citations. He shares the same eternal characteristic of the Godhead, yet there is no denying that His ministry had a distinct objective in Old Testament times. One major difference is that the Old Testament believers did not enjoy the indwelling ministry of the Holy Spirit as do believers today.

HIS WORKS TODAY

The unique ministry of the Holy Spirit for the New Testament period was announced by Jesus prior to the His death and resurrection. He promised the disciples that He would send them the comforter or advocate – the Holy Spirit (John 14:16 & 26, 16:7). He reiterated this

[3] Psalm 51:11; Isaiah 63:10–11
[4] Hodge, 1:527

immediately before His ascension (Acts 1:8), and the promise was fulfilled on the day of Pentecost, 50 days after His resurrection (Acts 2:1-4). This special ministry, which is expressly for the church today, is that of believers being actually indwelt and filled (empowered) with the Holy Spirit. No other time in history has there been a universal indwelling of the Holy Spirit made available to believers. The indwelling of the Spirit is permanent while the filling of the Spirit is a temporal ministry, which will be considered in the next chapter.

The following are the additional workings of the Holy Spirit today. The first two are specifically for the benefit of the unsaved.

1. *Convincing* – John 16:7-11

   This work of the Spirit to the unsaved is threefold:

   a. *Guilt in regard to sin* – i.e. the sin of unbelief in the reconciling work of Jesus Christ.
   b. *Righteousness* – to convince that the standard of right living before the Creator is the perfect life of the Lord Jesus Christ – the life which we are to imitate ("Put on the Lord Jesus Christ" – Romans 13:14).
   c. *Judgment to come* – because the triumph of the cross served notice to Satan and all who follow him of the certainty of eternal judgment for rejection of Christ.

   Dr. Chafer notes:

   > Much light falls upon the character of this essential ministry of the Holy Spirit when it is observed that the end which He accomplishes is the impartation of an understanding of facts, which understanding results in an enlightenment essential to an intelligent acceptance of Christ as Savior.[5]

2. *Restraining* – 2 Thessalonians 2:6-8

---

[5] Chafer, 6.33

According to Chafer, this ministry of the Spirit is directed to the whole world in order to restrain unbounded evil at the close of the present age. However, Chafer also states:

Evidently this curbing is not with a view to discontinuing all evil, else that would be accomplished without delay; it is rather a ministry by which evil is held within a certain divinely predetermined bounds.[6]

Geisler supports this and adds that:

The only person capable of restraining the kind of evil to be unleashed by the satanically inspired Antichrist is the Holy Spirit of God, whose indwelling presence in the body of believers will be taken away at the Rapture, before the horrendous period of Tribulation begins.[7]

3. *Regenerating* – John 3:5-6; Titus 3:5

The result of His work of conviction is regeneration – the act by which God, the Holy Spirit imparts eternal life.

4. *Interceding* – Romans 8:26-27

Scripture states that the Holy Spirit helps us with difficult prayer when we are under duress and may not know how to phrase our requests.

5. *Sanctifying* – 2 Thessalonians 2:13

The Holy Spirit supplies believers with the power to overcome evil, thus, separating them from unrighteousness and enabling them to glorifying God.

6. *Advocate* – John 14:16

While in the upper room, prior to Our Lord's death,

---

[6] Chafer, 6.34

[7] Geisler, 4.627. For a detailed discussion by Chafer in *Systematic Theology*, 6.85-88. Also, Pentecost, J. Dwight, *Things To Come* (1964) Grand Rapids, MI: Zondervan Publishing House, pp. 259-263

Jesus promised the disciples that He did not intend to leave them helpless in this world. He promised to ask the Father to send another like Himself who would be their advocate. The Holy Spirit is our counselor – One who assists us in the midst of trials and confrontations of this world. He is the One, as Dr. Vincent states:

…who suggests true reasonings to our minds, and true courses of action for our lives, who convicts our adversary, the world, of wrong, and pleads our cause before God our Father.[8]

And Dr. Chafer weighs in on this matter, quoting William Kelley that the Holy Spirit is:

"…but one who is identified with our interests, one who undertakes all our cause, one who engages to see us through our difficulties, one who in every way becomes both our representative and the great personal agent that transacts all our business for us."[9]

7. *Illumination* – John 16:13; 1 Corinthians 2:10

The Apostle Paul asserts that the minds of mankind have been veiled by Satan from understanding spiritual phenomenon.[10] It is therefore the role of the Holy Spirit to guide believers into "all truth" and make known to them "things to come" in the future.

This special ministry to believers is designed so that *all* believers will be able to comprehend the doctrines of the Christian faith.[11] Dr. Chafer points out that regarding the believer:

The divine Teacher [the Holy Spirit] is within his heart and he therefore does not hear a voice speaking from

---

[8] Vincent, 2.244
[9] Chafer, 6.39
[10] 2 Corinthians 4:3-4 cp/w 1 Corinthians 2:14
[11] Ephesians 3:18

without…but the mind and heart are supernaturally awakened from within to apprehend what otherwise would be unknown.[12]

8. *Giving of gifts* – Romans 12:4-8; 1 Corinthians 12:4-11; Ephesians 4:7-11; 1 Peter 4:10-11

Scripture states that the Holy Spirit bestows gifts to each believer:

But to each one is given the manifestation of the Spirit for the common good…But one and the same Spirit works all these things, distributing to each one individually just as He wills. (1 Corinthians 12:7, 11)

These gifts are designed to make evident the indwelling Holy Spirit in the life of the believer. It is a means of providing essential spiritual services to believers while presenting a unified and dynamic witness before the world.

In defining this ministry of the Holy Spirit, Dr. Chafer writes:

It may be said that a gift in the spiritual sense means the Holy Spirit doing a particular service through the believer and using the believer to do it.[13]

This appears to be the accepted view in Christianity today, except Chafer goes on to claim that the entire working of the believer's gift is wholly a demonstration of the Spirit's efforts unaided by the believer.

It is not something the believer is doing by the aid of the Holy Spirit, nor is it a mere augmentation of what is termed a native or natural gift. According to 1 Corinthians 12:7, a gift is a "manifestation of the Spirit." It is conceivable that the Spirit might use native

---

[12] Chafer, 1.109
[13] Chafer, 6.216

gifts, but the gift which is wrought by the Spirit is an expression of His own ability rather than the mere use of human qualities in the one through whom He works.[14]

The Holy Spirit then works in and through the life of the believer in order to make Himself and His power known to the believer as well as to the world.

The gifts that He bestows upon believers vary in importance (Pastor–teacher, evangelist, apostles), temporal (sign gifts: tongues, miracles, healings), and those that are enduring (wisdom, faith, mercy, giving, helps). There is no Scriptural evidence that spiritual maturity is defined by the type of gift that one has been bestowed. One of the major problems in the church today is the elevating of the pastor to a status far above the people in the pews. The reality is that the gift of the Pastor-teacher is indeed an extremely important function in the church deserving of respectful attention to the content of what he teaches. However, the attempt to divide the church into clergy and laity is contrary to clear Scriptural teachings. Paul wrote specifically of this when he said "we are God's fellow workers."[15]

Spiritual maturity in the early years of the church, during the first century, was determined by the degree of love, faith, and hope that was being demonstrated by believers. Paul wrote:

But now faith, hope, love, abide these three; but the greatest of these is love. (1 Corinthians 13:13)

Paul's emphasis on this concept of love is a recurring theme of his and other New Testament writers.[16] These

---

[14] Chafer, 6.216

[15] 1 Corinthians 3:9

[16] Getz notes that it "appears over fifty times in the Epistles alone," *Sharpen-*

three virtues – faith, hope and love – are enduring and should be developed by all believers in order to manifest a life of Godliness.[17]

CONCLUSION

A careful and discerning study is required to comprehend the Biblical doctrine of the Holy Spirit. Scripture affirms the reality of His person and that He possesses all of the attributes of deity. He is not, as some have imagined, merely a New Testament personage, but appears in the Old Testament in many passages.

The work of the Holy Spirit in this dispensation is unique from all other ages. For everyone who trusts in Christ is indwelt and empowered by the Holy Spirit. Each are baptized with His identifying 'mark' that they are Christ's. Some of His distinctive ministries include: the regeneration of all believers, intercession in prayer, illumination of Scripture, and the provision of specialized gifts.

The Christians' life has been enriched beyond measure because of the unique mentorship ministry of the Holy Spirit. Exploiting all that He has to offer is a key factor for the believer to advance and reach his spiritual growth potential.

---

ing The Focus of the Church, (1974) Chicago, IL: Moody, pp. 114-116

[17] For a broader discussion of Spiritual Gifts see: Geisler, Norman (2005) *Systematic Theology*, Minneapolis, MN: Bethany House, 4.187-202

CHAPTER CHECK

1. What are the proofs that the Holy Spirit is a person?

2. Describe the attributes of deity of the Holy Spirit.

3. What are some of the Old Testament evidences of the Holy Spirit?

4. Explain the work of the Holy Spirit today.

5. How does His work today affect you?

6. What are some of the gifts of the Holy Spirit?

7. Is there a hierarchy of gifts for the church today?

❧ 8 ❧

THE DOCTRINE OF MAN AND SIN

MAN'S ORIGIN

Scripture states in Genesis:

> Then God said, "Let Us make man in Our image, according to Our likeness; and let them rule over the fish of the sea and over the birds of the sky and over the cattle and over all the earth, and over every creeping thing that creeps on the earth." God created man in His own image, in the image of God He created him; male and female He created them. God blessed them; and God said to them, "Be fruitful and multiply, and fill the earth, and subdue it; and rule over the fish of the sea and over the birds of the sky and over every living thing that moves on the earth." [1]

This passage describes the event that took place on the 6th day of creation. Biblical Christianity maintains that the Genesis account is an accurate description of God's creative activity. Christianity believes in the authority and accuracy of Scripture to the extent that if one could travel back in a time machine to the moment in time of man's creation, that this event could be recorded with a digital movie camera precisely as described in the Genesis account. One

---

[1] Genesis 1:26-28

could see and preserve digitally the mighty work of the Creator as He "formed man from the dust of the ground, and breathed into his nostrils the breath of life; and the man became a living being."[2] For in this work of creation, God gives to man life with the intention of having fellowship with Him.

He made man in His own image.[3] This is the major point of differentiation between man and the rest of creation. Man's significance lies in the fact that he alone in the entire universe was created in the image of God. This sets up the true picture of man in the universe: that he is the creature of the Creator. This does not imply that man is insignificant. Instead, it is a magnificent position that he holds in the created universe. It means that man has a Creator who desired to have a personal relationship with His creatures. To blur the Creator/creature distinction is to truly belittle God and to diminish His creation. This is what is at issue in our culture today. Man does not recognize his true significance in the universe because of his rejection of this truth and his rejection of the God of the universe. This rebellious attitude is described by the Apostle Paul as a suppression of the truth.[4] The objective of the rebellious ones is to attempt, by any means, to disprove the Scriptures concerning the God of this universe.

A good example of this is the book *The Origin of Species* (1859) by Charles Darwin, published over 150 years ago. In His book Darwin explains his theory of the evolution of all species, including man. This open rejection of the creation account in Genesis has attempted to turn Biblical Christianity inside-out. Many Christians have been deceived by this seemingly convincing theory. They have been intimidated by a God-less culture, and have attempted to either harmonize Scripture with scientific theories or to completely disregard the Biblical account of creation. For the Christian, the refutation of the evolution theory should be relatively straightforward. First of all, it is simply a *theory,* and one which is destitute of any concluding factuality. Even Darwin admitted that it was deficient because of a

---

[2] Genesis 2:7 NRSV
[3] Genesis 1:27
[4] Romans 1:18

"missing link."[5] Secondly, the Christian must ask the question: by whose authority do we arrive at truth – man's or God's? If we choose man's authority, than we allow those who presuppose that there is no Creator to lead us into their beliefs. If we choose God's authority, we have absolute truth in explaining all of His works of creation. If we choose man's authority, we call Jesus a liar, for He stated concerning the Word of God, "Your word is truth."[6] If we call Jesus a liar, than we have no source of truth, no salvation, and no purpose for life. The disbelief of this extraordinary work of the Creator creating man in His own image has attributed to the momentous despair which we see in our culture and the manic search for anything and everything that can make one happy.

MAN'S PURPOSE

If indeed God created man in His own image, then what is the meaning of life, or more precisely, what is the purpose of man?

The first question of the Westminster Confession states that:

> Man's chief and highest end is to glorify God, (Rom. 11:36, 1 Cor. 10:31) and fully to enjoy him forever. (Ps. 73:24–28, John 17:21–23)[7]

This is a truth that is so often ignored, even within Christian circles. The original purpose for which God created man in His own image was to glorify Him and to enjoy his fellowship in the garden forever. However, man fell from this state of grace because of his sin of rebellion, and his purpose cannot be fully realized apart from being reconciled to his Creator by the finished work of Christ on the cross.

It is the objective of the Creator to seek man out and to save him; to restore him to his rightful place of greatness in His universe. And

---

[5] Darwin, C. R. (1859) *The Origin of Species*, London: W. Clowers & Sons, pp. 279-280

[6] John 17:17

[7] *The Westminster Larger Catechism* (1996) Oak Harbor, WA: Logos Research Systems, Inc., Question 1

He has accomplished this through the sacrificial death of His Son, Jesus Christ.

> For it was the Father's good pleasure for all the fullness to dwell in Him, and through Him to reconcile all things to Himself, having made peace through the blood of His cross. (Colossians 1:19-20a)

The consequence of the fall provides the basis for the Christian's message to a lost world of their need to make peace with the Creator. Believers are given the responsibility to spread the Gospel to all men so that they might be reconciled with their Creator and to glorify Him.

MAN AND SIN

Man is a complex being, consisting of body, soul and spirit. The body, as we have seen from Genesis 2:7, God formed from the dust of the earth. However, the soul and spirit are the immaterial parts of man. Chafer states:

> Soul connotes that in the immaterial part of man which is related to life, action, emotion. Spirit is that part within related to worship, communion, divine influence.[8]

Just as God breathed into Adam nostrils the breath of life, the new born child's first breath is that of God's impartation of the soul and spirit into their physical body. The soul being that part of man which is who he is; the spirit is that part of man designed to commune with his Creator.

However, man is unable to have meaningful fellowship with his Creator, for the Scriptures declare that men are born spiritually dead as a result of the imputation of Adam's sin.

> Therefore, just as through one man [Adam] sin entered into the world, and death through sin, and so death spread to all men, because all sinned. (Romans 5:12)

---

[8] Chafer, 7.291

Since God is holy and righteous, He cannot fellowship with those who are not holy and righteous. Therefore, sin creates a barrier between God and man.

He goes further in describing the former estate of the believer:

> And you were dead in your trespasses and sins, in which you formerly walked according to the course of this world, according to the prince of the power of the air, of the spirit that is now working in the sons of disobedience. Among them we too all formerly lived in the lusts of our flesh, indulging the desires of the flesh and of the mind, and were by nature children of wrath, even as the rest. (Ephesians 2:1-3)

It is a picture of man totally corrupted by the "course of this world" controlled by Satan, "the prince of the power of the air."

Man is unable to make amends with his Creator, for Paul says that man's salvation is not "a result of works."[9] Modern man understands this emptiness, the loss of his true identity with his Creator and instead of acknowledging the truth of the Gospel he suppresses the truth in unrighteousness.[10]

Paul understood the despair of mankind, the same despair that is in our culture of disbelief. We live in a culture of men, who do not understand their real purpose in the universe of their Creator; oblivious to their higher purpose – to glorify God. Modern man tries everything to satiate the emptiness; filling their minds with whatever will soothe the inner pangs of desperation: careers, education, toys, sex, amusements.

The consequence of unbelief is that men will spend eternity separated from their Creator. But God has demonstrated His love and mercy by providing the means by which man can regain his place of fellowship with his Creator. This was His original intention for creating man in His image, to provide a meaningful and noble purpose for existence.

---

[9] Ephesians 2:9; Titus 3:5
[10] Romans 1:18ff

CONCLUSION

Scripture concludes that God created man in His image, to glorify Him and for man to enjoy his Creator forever. He designed man to be a creature nobler than the birds and the beast – for man was able to fellowship with his Creator. However, because of the disobedience of Adam, man fell from his lofty position. Sin caused a barrier between him and his Creator, necessitating a means to resolve his predicament.

Men through the ages have attempted to relieve the anxiety of their lost and sinful condition. They have sought frantically to discover the real purpose of their existence in temporal things, while suppressing the truth of the impediment of sin separating them from their Creator. In all their efforts, they are unable to break down the barrier.

But thanks to the grace and mercy of God the Father, He has provided the solution for man by the substitutionary death of His Son, Jesus Christ.

CHAPTER CHECK

1. How does Scripture describe man's beginning?

2. In what way does man possess the image of God?

3. Explain the refutation of the creation account of man.

4. What is man's chief purpose?

5. What are the immaterial parts of man?

6. What was God's original design for man?

7. Describe how the unbeliever rejects God.

ও 9 ৫

THE DOCTRINE OF SALVATION

Before establishing the biblical definition of salvation it would be worthwhile to consider one of the most profound misconceptions regarding God's glorious provision of salvation in some circles of Christianity today. Namely, that salvation is an easy pass to elude the fires of Hell. Although it is true that those who accept Christ as their Savior do indeed escape eternal punishment in the Lake of Fire, God's salvation is *not* merely fire insurance.

Neither is salvation something that an individual gives assent to in order, as it were, to "cover his bets" and to place Jesus alongside his acknowledgment of Buddha, Allah, Baal, Krishna or the entire pantheon of Greek and Roman gods. Man was created a rational being in God's image, so it follows that the free gift of salvation is something that is to be understood intellectually. What follows is an attempt to provide a Biblical examination of the subject.

SALVATION DEFINED

Dr. Chafer provides a good working definition of salvation.

> According to its largest meaning used in Scripture, the word "salvation" represents the whole work of God by which He rescues man from *the eternal ruin and doom of sin* and

bestows on him the riches of His grace, including eternal life now and eternal glory in heaven. [emphasis added][1]

Elsewhere he explains further:

This larger use of the word, therefore, combines in it many separate works of God for the individual, such as Atonement, Grace, Propitiation, Forgiveness, Justification, Imputation, Regeneration, Adoption, Sanctification, Redemption and Glorification.[2]

A careful study of these separate works of God reveals that His overall objective in salvation is to provide man a means by which he can be reconciled once and for all with his Creator. The means by which this is accomplished is through the substitutionary death of Jesus Christ on the cross for the forgiveness of all the sins of mankind.[3] It should be clarified that God is not in need being reconciled with man, it is man who needs to be reconciled to God.

Therefore the divine work of God in salvation was accomplished by the finished work of Christ on the cross in order to reconcile man with his Creator and rescued him from the eternal ruin and doom of sin.

Is Salvation Necessary?

Paul states the basic need of salvation when he wrote:

For all have sinned and fall short of the glory of God. (Romans 3:23)

Sin is the barrier which separates man and God. Since God is holy, He is unable to have fellowship with His creatures. This takes us back to the origin of sin, back to Genesis and the Fall of Adam and Eve (Genesis 3). When Eve succumbed to the temptation of the serpent and Adam flagrantly disobeyed God's command prohibiting

---

[1] Chafer, Lewis Sperry (1974) *Major Bible Themes*, Grand Rapids, MI: Zondervan, p. 181

[2] Chafer, Lewis Sperry (1991) *Salvation: God's Marvelous Work of Grace*, Grand Rapids, MI: Kregel, pp. 13-14

[3] 1 John 2:2; Luke 1:77; Hebrews 9:22

them to eat anything from the tree of the knowledge of good and evil (Genesis 2:17), sin entered the human race. Sin has been described as "missing the mark." But in reality, sin is man's rebellious disobedience and rejection of the authority of his Creator. John describes sin as lawlessness (1 John 3:4). It is what causes men to be spiritually dead – which is separation from a holy God. David stated in Psalm 51:5 that he was "brought forth in iniquity," a sinful condition. Paul quotes David concerning the disposition of all men:

> There is none righteous, not even one;
> There is none who understands,
> There is none who seeks for God;
> All have turned aside, together they have become useless;
> There is none who does good,
> There is not even one. (Romans 3:10-12)

Scripture therefore portrays all men as "sons of disobedience" (Ephesians 2:2) and equally in need of salvation.

THE GOOD NEWS

Usually, before there is good news there is bad news. In this case the bad news is the fact that all men are sinners and in need of salvation. Plus, to add pain to misery, there is *nothing* that a man can do in order to be reconciled with his Creator. Not by penance, not by a system of prayer and neither will good works make man acceptable to God. Isaiah wrote that the Divine viewpoint is that "all of our righteous deeds are like a filthy garment" (Isaiah 64:6). Most people discard filthy garments, and so does God. Paul concurs with Isaiah's opinion when he wrote to Titus:

> He saved us, not on the basis of deeds which we have done in righteousness. (Titus 3:5)

This leads to the good news. But first note the condition that man is in when he comes to God. Paul ascribes to the Ephesians this condition – it is the same dreadful condition that all men find themselves:

> And you were dead in your trespasses and sins, in which you formerly walked according to the course of this world,

according to the prince of the power of the air, of the spirit that is now working in the sons of disobedience. Among them we too all formerly lived in the lusts of our flesh, indulging the desires of the flesh and of the mind, and were by nature children of wrath, even as the rest. (Ephesians 2:1-3)

And then Paul relates the good news beginning with the two of the most wonderful words in Scripture:

But God, being rich in mercy, because of His great love with which He loved us, even when we were dead in our transgressions, made us alive together with Christ (by grace you have been saved). [emphasis added] (Ephesians 2:4-5)

But only God could find a way to save mankind from consequence of sin, and He did so through the work of His Son, Jesus Christ on the cross. This is the good news, the Gospel of salvation. Paul explains it concisely to the Corinthians:

Now I make known to you, brethren, the gospel which I preached to you, which also you received, in which also you stand, by which also you are saved, if you hold fast the word which I preached to you, unless you believed in vain. For I delivered to you as of first importance what I also received, that Christ died for our sins according to the Scriptures, and that He was buried, and that He was raised on the third day according to the Scriptures. (1 Corinthians 15:1-4)

This is the Gospel precisely stated. It is the only truth by which sinful man can find reconciliation with his Creator. Please note that Paul supports his truth statements concerning the relevant facts of the Gospel, the death, burial, and resurrection of Jesus Christ, upon the foundations of Scriptures. These truths are indisputable prophesies found in the writings of the Old Testament. Paul provides us with an apt demonstration of the foundation upon which all of our beliefs in the Christian faith rest – Scripture.

The Objective of the Gospel

God's purpose in providing the sacrifice of His Son on the cross as already stated was to provide man with a means to regain fellowship with his Creator both now and for eternity. Scripture states that His divine desire is that "all men be saved and come to the knowledge of the truth" (1 Timothy 2:4). How else could John state with conviction:

> For God so loved the world that He gave His only begotten Son, that whoever believes in Him shall not perish, but have eternal life. (John 3:16)

Peter concurred as he wrote concerning the coming judgment to end the ages:

> The Lord is not slow about His promise, as some count slowness, but is patient toward you, not wishing for any to perish but for all to come to repentance. (2 Peter 3:9)

There is a distinct desire of the Creator to provide all of mankind with a means to restore their relationship with Him. Scripture is clear that there is nothing that man can do; no restitution that he can provide that would mend this broken relationship. And further there is no one who seeks after God. But God (as Paul stated) has reached out to His creatures and provided a way. And, His way is an offer which is made available to "whoever believes in Him."

THE MECHANICS OF THE GOSPEL

For men to be reconciled with their Creator, they must believe in the truth statements of the Gospel that:

> Christ died for our sins according to the Scriptures, and that He was buried, and that He was raised on the third day according to the Scriptures. (1 Corinthians 15:3-4)

When the jailer in Philippi asked Paul and Silas what he must do to be saved, they stated in the simplest terms:

> Believe in the Lord Jesus, and you will be saved, you and your household. (Acts 16:31)

It is this simple expression of faith (no works required) which Paul explains in the Epistle to the Ephesians:

> For by grace you have been saved through faith; and that not of yourselves, it is the gift of God; not as a result of works, so that no one may boast. (Ephesians 2:8-9)

Paul in quoting Isaiah states that "whoever believes in Him will not be disappointed."[4] This is exactly how Chafer defines faith, as "personal confidence in God."[5] A God who is truthful and reliable; one in whom we should put our faith and trust in, based upon the provision of salvation that He offers.

So where does this faith come from? Paul asks this same question:

> How then will they call on Him in whom they have not believed? How will they believe in Him whom they havenot heard? (Romans 10:14)

It presupposes that in order for someone to believe they must first hear the Gospel message. This implies that a person's thought process must make an intelligent decision. For true faith is *not* a leap into the unknown, with the hope that what is believed *might* be true. It is a confident reliance upon God Who is known to be trustworthy, and has demonstrated this characteristic throughout Scripture in His dealings with mankind.

Faith is a gift of God and, as Paul states further in Romans, faith "comes from hearing, and hearing by the word of Christ."[6] And this presents a challenge to the Christian of the 21st Century, to provide a hearing of this Gospel of salvation in order to challenge men to trust Christ as their Savior.

THE HINDRANCE TO THE GOSPEL

There is a hindrance that poses a challenge for the Christian in

---

4   Romans 9:33
5   Chafer, 7.146
6   Romans 10:17

providing Gospel hearing to the lost: Satan's world order. Satan's work of obstructing the spread of God's provision of salvation has not stopped since his work began in the Garden of Eden. Paul wrote to the Corinthians concerning this:

> And even if our gospel is veiled, it is veiled to those who are perishing, in whose case the god of this world has blinded the minds of the unbelieving so that they might not see the light of the gospel of the glory of Christ, who is the image of God. (2 Corinthians 4:3-4)

The solution for believers today is to persist in their collaborated resistance to the evil schemes of Satan and his demons. Of course this implies that we accept the Scripture's literal revelation concerning the god of this world. Paul affirms this in his Epistle to the Ephesians:

> For our struggle is not against flesh and blood, but against the rulers, against the powers, against the world forces of this darkness, against the spiritual forces of wickedness in the heavenly places. (Ephesians 6:12)

Paul instructs us to be equipped with the necessary armament provided us: the Word of God and the empowering Holy Spirit. We must not forget that: "Greater is He who is in us, than he who is in the world"[7] and we must continue to present this Gospel of salvation to all men, even in the midst of great opposition.

THE POWER OF THE GOSPEL

The Apostle Paul loved the message of the Gospel, and was eager[8] and willing to communicate its truth by his writings and preaching. Everywhere he traveled, he spoke of the reality of the death and resurrection of Jesus Christ. He explained the reason for his confidence in the Gospel message:

> For I am not ashamed of the gospel, for it is the power of God for salvation to everyone who believes, to the Jew first and also to the Greek. (Romans 1:16)

---

[7] 1 John 4:4
[8] Romans 1:15

In last half of the 20ᵗʰ Century two things happened that changed the thinking of many Christians. First, there was the question of Lordship. Many believed that if a sinner did not accept Jesus as both his Lord *and* savior, then he was not saved. The problem that this issue attempted to solve was the impression of a simple and undemanding Gospel. In other words, a person could merely make a statement of faith in Christ as savior and then go out and live as if nothing ever happened and still go to heaven after he died. But in reality, when a sinner hears the Gospel and trusts in Christ, he really has no choice in the matter since Christ *is* the Lord *and* savior. The real problem was that the message of the Gospel had not been clearly communicated. When a person accepts Christ as their savior, it should be stressed that it is not fire insurance. That they have been reconciled with their Creator and are now entering into the relationship which God had intended originally for every man. And this relationship is to be lived in a holy manner or the consequence would be discipline from the Father.

Secondly, Christianity seemed to have forgotten an important aspect of the Gospel, namely, that it is the power of God for salvation.

Dr. Wuest comments concerning this power:

> Of the six words for "power" in the Greek language, Paul chooses *dunamis* [δυναμις] to describe the effectual working of the good news of salvation. *Dunamis* is power, natural ability, inherent power residing in a thing by virtue of its nature, or, power which a person or thing exerts or puts forth. The gospel is the inherent, omnipotent power of God operating in the salvation of a lost soul that accepts it.[9]

Therefore, within the actual message of the Gospel resides God's power for salvation. It stands to reason then, that the message must be understood by the unbeliever. Once that is accomplished, God's operating power for salvation completes its objective of reconciling the unbeliever to Him.

Vincent states that the gospel is:

---

[9] Wuest, Vol. I, "Romans," p. 24

> Not merely a powerful means in God's hands, but in itself
> a divine energy. [10]

It is instructive for those who present the Gospel to the unbeliever to recognize that inherent in the message is the power of God for salvation. What this means is that the Christian needs to do nothing more than present the specifics of the Gospel. Adding a personal testimony, a story, a particular vocal modulation, a provocation of fear, or any other human device is unnecessary, because the real power for conviction comes from within the message of the Gospel. As Wuest points out, "It is the good news of salvation energized by the Holy Spirit."[11]

We must remember that, as in all of God's workings, the provision of salvation is the grace of God at work, in all of its aspects. Human viewpoint dictates that the Gospel ought to be presented in a certain manner in order to get the desired results; divine viewpoint states that the Gospel message is the power of God for salvation. This doesn't mean that the believer should disregard the timing and the occasion of when he witnesses. For instance, doing it during working hours would be highly inappropriate. What it does mean is that believers should be thoroughly knowledgeable of the Gospel message and totally reliant upon its intrinsic power.

CONCLUSION

The doctrine of salvation states that all men are dead in their sins and are in need of salvation. This need is so that they might be reconciled with their Creator and enjoy eternal fellowship with Him. This is the missing element in every man which makes him incomplete as a person – his relationship with his Creator, as it was originally intended by God. It has been illustrated that man does not seek after God on his own initiative, so that God must find a way to accomplish His objective of saving mankind. And He did so by the substitutionary death of His Son, Jesus Christ, on the cross. His offer of salvation is made to all who will believe. But in order for

---

[10] Vincent, 3.9
[11] Wuest, Vol. I, "Romans," p. 24

them to express faith in Christ as their Savior, they must first hear His Gospel of salvation. Once he hears this message of salvation, he must decide if he is to accept this grace gift from God. There is nothing that a man can do as far as working to gain merit to earn this gift – Christ has done it all. Men must now express faith and confidence in the trustworthy God of the universe, in His plan that redeems him of his sin through the cross of Christ in order to attain reconciliation with his Creator, to be at peace with Him and to enjoy His fellowship forever.

There are many other areas that could have been discussed in this section concerning salvation, for instance, the theological terms: Justification, sanctification, reconciliation, propitiation, redemption, imputation, and regeneration. These are very important subjects; however they reach beyond the scope of this study. The student of the Word should direct his attention to these studies in theology as noted in the bibliography.

CHAPTER CHECK

1. What is the Biblical meaning of salvation?

2. Why did God provide a means for salvation?

3. Upon what basis does Paul support the truth of the Gospel?

4. Explain the mechanics of the Gospel?

5. What is God's desire concerning all men?

6. How does Satan hinder the Gospel?

7. What should be our attitude concerning the opposition to our witnessing?

8. What is meant by the power of the Gospel?

❧ 10 ❧

THE DOCTRINE OF THE END TIMES

The doctrine concerning the End Times is also known as "Things to Come", the "Last Things" and in theology as the study of Eschatology.[1] The study of the end times has been a matter of interest for believers since the 1st Century. Our Lord's disciples showed great interest when they asked Jesus what would be the sign of His coming again and the end of the age.[2] His answer to them was extensive, taking up the whole of chapters 24 and 25 of Matthew's Gospel. The Apostle Paul wrote to the Thessalonians concerning the end times because they worried that their departed loved ones would fail to benefit from the blessed event of Christ's return for His church. Paul assured them that they would not miss out and also described the events surrounding Christ's return for believers in what is known as the Rapture of the Church.[3] In the latter part of the 20th Century there was an increased awareness of Biblical prophecy producing writers and teachers such as Dr. Jack Van Impe, Hal Lindsey and the widely popular "Left Behind" series of books and movies by Tim LaHaye and Jerry Jenkins.[4] Even now there are

---

[1] The full scope of Eschatology is concerned with unfulfilled as well as fulfilled prophesy. The "end times" typically involves the prophetic events which are yet future.

[2] Matthew 24:3

[3] 1 Thessalonians 4:13-18; see also 2 Thessalonians 2.

[4] Note that this had not been true in the early part of the 20th Century.

renewed prophetic interests as the year 2012 approaches, specifically concerning the Mayan calendar's claim of a cataclysmic end of the world and the prophecies of the 16th Century French physician and astrologer Michel Nostradamus.

Some believer's have become obsessed and overly fixated with the Biblical subject of prophecy. There should be caution taken when approaching any study of God's Word not to excessively stress one segment of doctrine over the rest of God's teaching. One must remember that *all* Scripture is profitable for the equipping of the believer.[5]

The intent here is to provide a logical outline of events concerning the end times: The Rapture of the Church of Jesus Christ; the period of Tribulation; Christ's Second Coming; His Millennial Kingdom on earth; the end of the Kingdom age; the Judgments; and the Eternal state. This subject of the end times is one of the most controversial subjects in Christianity along with the deity of Christ, the nature of spirituality, and the inspiration and authority of Scripture. The Christian's beliefs concerning the end times will determine how he views the world today and what his responsibilities and endeavors are for Christian service.

The Background

Before describing the events of the end times, there is a need to look at what has transpired so far in the plan of God for the ages. Without an understanding of what has already occurred so far with God's plan for mankind, there is the potential for great misunderstanding of His ultimate plans for the human race and His desired involvement of believers within His plan.

To begin with, God in His supreme wisdom has provided through His Word a means by which His plan can be understood in its

---

Chafer wrote that "many theologians have from the first given themselves to the study of Soteriology almost exclusively, to the all-but-complete neglect of Eschatology." *Systematic Theology*, 7.139

[5] 2 Timothy 3:16-17

logical order. There is a clear demarcation within the historical record of Scripture of distinct periods of time. These periods have become known as dispensations. Dr. C. I. Scofield's definition of dispensation:

> A dispensation is a period of time during which man is tested in respect of obedience to some *specific* revelation of the will of God. Seven such dispensations are distinguished in Scripture. [emphasis his][6]

It is not within the scope of this study to describe and explain the various dispensations of the God's plan and purpose for mankind.[7] It should be carefully noted that the study of dispensations is not a doctrine. Instead, it is a principle of interpretation that assists the student of the Word in differentiating God's relationship with His believers and with mankind throughout history. An understanding of dispensations *is* pertinent to the study of the end times because it clarifies the distinctions in God's plan and purpose for Gentiles, Israel and the Church. The aim is to understand who comprises these factions and exactly what role they play in the final culmination of God's plan and program for the ages.

There were no designated peoples to represent God within the nations of mankind prior to God's calling of Abram to become the father of the nation of Israel. These groups of nations were known subsequently as the Nations or the Gentiles. The Greek scholar Spiros Zodhiates comments that:

> In the Jewish sense the nations, means the Gentile nations or the Gentiles in general as spoken of all who are not Israelites and implying idolatry and ignorance of the true God, i.e., the heathen, pagan nations [8]

The nations of the world were indeed heathen and pagan in their attitudes towards the God of the universe in the ensuing years after

---

[6] Scofield, C. I. (1945) *The Scofield Study Bible*, New York, NY: Oxford University Press, p. 5, *note* 4

[7] An excellent book on the subject of Dispensations is: Ryrie, C. C. (1995) *Dispensationalism*, Chicago, IL: Moody Press.

[8] Zodhiates, G1484

the universal flood from which Noah and his family was rescued in the Ark. This is evidenced in the highlighted events of the Tower of Babel (Genesis 11:1-9) and the destruction of the cities of Sodom and Gomorrah (Genesis 18:16 – 19:38). The failure of the heads of nations and families to make known and to honor the Creator prompted God to set apart a nation to witness to all mankind of His existence and of His glory.

Israel became the people of God. The relationship of God with His people was based upon a series of covenants: Abrahamic (Genesis 12:1-7); Mosaic (Exodus 19); Palestinian (Deuteronomy 30:1-10); Davidic (2 Samuel 7:12-16); New (Jeremiah 31:31-34). Some of the covenant provisions were conditioned upon the faithfulness of Israel and would not be fulfilled if Israel failed to uphold their end of the agreement. However, some were unconditional covenants, and God was and is obligated to fulfill His promises based upon His integrity. Specifically looking at the Palestinian covenant there are many unfulfilled provisions. Dr. Pentecost observes:

> Israel must be converted as a nation, must be regathered from her world-wide dispersion, must be installed in her land, which she is made to possess, must witness the judgment of her enemies, and must receive the material blessings vouchsafed to her.[9]

Since God is not a liar or one to go back on His word, Israel will have a future fulfillment of all the unconditional provisions of the Palestinian covenant. This fact indeed will have much to bear in this study of the end times.

The Bible makes a distinction about another group of people called the Church; the Body of Jesus Christ, true believers in the God of the Bible and the focal point of His plan today. Because of the rejection by Israel of their Messiah, Jesus Christ, God called out a group who would be comprised of both Jews and Gentiles to become His witnesses in the world until His return for them prior to the end of this age. Chapter 2 detailed the nature and composition of the

---

[9] Pentecost, pp. 98-99.

Church and that the Church has a primary position today in God's plan as well as a destiny in the final days and in the eternal state.

There is absolute Scriptural support demonstrating the differences in God's dealings with each of these factions in history: Gentiles, Israel, and the Church. It does not make God inconsistent, neither does it demonstrate that His character changes. For in all of His dealings with mankind He in no way compromises His holy and eternal characteristics.

THE RAPTURE OF THE CHURCH

The Apostle Paul spoke of this present Church age as "the mystery which for ages has been hidden in God who created all things" (Ephesians 3:9). It is described to be an *intercalary* period – that is, a period of time inserted into another age. There is ample Scriptural evidence that the present Church age has been inserted into the age of Israel, interrupting the 70 Weeks prophecy of Daniel 9.[10] In addition to the previously stated fact that God has not fulfilled all of the provisions of the covenants with His people, Daniel along with Old and New Testament citations, prophesied of a coming judgment upon the nation Israel, one that has not been witnessed at any time in history. Jeremiah wrote:

> Alas! for that day is great,
> There is none like it;
> And it is the time of Jacob's distress,
> But he will be saved from it. (Jeremiah 30:7)

Zephaniah wrote:

> Near is the great day of the Lord,
> Near and coming very quickly;
> Listen, the day of the Lord!
> In it the warrior cries out bitterly.
> A day of wrath is that day,
> A day of trouble and distress,

---

[10] Daniel 9:24-27

A day of destruction and desolation,
A day of darkness and gloom,
A day of clouds and thick darkness. (Zephaniah 1:14-15)

Jesus also spoke of this coming tribulation also:

> For then there will be a great tribulation, such as has not occurred since the beginning of the world until now, nor ever will. (Matthew 24:21)[11]

But before Israel's covenant provisions are fulfilled and their coming tribulation, the Church will be removed in what has become known as the Rapture of the Church. The term "rapture" comes from the verb in the Latin Bible which translates the phrase "shall be caught up" in 1 Thessalonians 4:17.[12] It literally means a snatching away.

The fact of this occurrence is based upon a literal interpretation of applicable passages of Scripture. Paul writing to the Thessalonians provides a clear description of the event:

> But we do not want you to be uninformed, brethren, about those who are asleep, so that you will not grieve as do the rest who have no hope. For if we believe that Jesus died and rose again, even so God will bring with Him those who have fallen asleep in Jesus. For this we say to you by the word of the Lord, that we who are alive and remain until the coming of the Lord, will not precede those who have fallen asleep. For the Lord Himself will descend from heaven with a shout, with the voice of the archangel and with the trumpet of God, and the dead in Christ will rise first. Then we who are alive and remain will be caught up together with them in the clouds to meet the Lord in the air, and so we shall always be with the Lord. Therefore comfort one another with these words. (1 Thessalonians 4:13-18)

---

[11] See further: Luke 21:25-26; 1 Thessalonians 5:3; Revelation 3:10, 6:15-17

[12] MacDonald, W., & Farstad, A. (1997, c1995) Believer's *Bible Commentary: Old and New Testaments* (electronic ed.) (1 Th 4:17). Nashville, TN: Thomas Nelson.

First, Paul states that when the Lord Jesus comes, God will bring *with* Him those who have fallen asleep.[13] Secondly, he says in verse 17 that we who are alive and remain will be caught up *together with them* in the clouds. Living believers will be caught up together with those church age believers who have died before this event because Paul stated in verse 16 that "the dead in Christ will rise first."

The last part of verse 17 is what has been termed as Our Blessed Hope – "and so we shall always be with the Lord." The believers of this age have an eternal hope which is in the "heavenly places"[14] with the Lord Jesus Christ, for all eternity.

When Jesus Christ returns for His church, He will only meet them *in* the air and will not descend *to* the earth. Although He will eventually return to the earth, this event should not be confused with the yet future event known as His Second Coming.

The fact of the Rapture having been established by Paul in 1st Thessalonians logically leads us to the promise that the church will be gone from the earth prior to the coming Tribulation period, which completes the age of Israel. This Rapture promise can be found in three passages: 1 Thessalonians 1:9-10, 5:9 and Revelation 3:10.

In Paul's introductory remarks in 1st Thessalonians he commends them for their awaiting the return of Jesus Christ, who, he adds, "rescues us from the wrath to come (1:10)." The "wrath to come" is a reference to the Tribulation period coming upon the entire world. He reiterates this in chapter 5, verse 9: "For God has not destined us for wrath, but for obtaining salvation through the Lord Jesus Christ." And then in verse 10, Paul again underscores the fact inferred in chapter 4, verse 17, that "whether we are awake or asleep [dead], we will live together with Him."

The Apostle John in the book of Revelation, records the promise made by the Lord Jesus Christ to the church at Philadelphia in Asia for their faithfulness in keeping His Word. Jesus is quoted:

[13] "Fallen asleep" is a Biblical reference to a believer's death, cp/w Matthew 27:52; John 11:11; Acts 7:60; 13:36; 1 Corinthians 11:30; 15:6, 18, 20, 51; 2 Peter 3:4.
[14] Ephesians 2:6

> Because you have kept the word of My perseverance, I also will keep you from the hour of testing, that hour which is about to come upon the whole world, to test those who dwell on the earth. (Revelation 3:10)

It should be emphasized that the church is here assured that it will be kept *from* the hour of testing. According to A.T. Robertson, a New Testament Greek grammarian, the Greek preposition translated in this verse "from" conveys the "idea of separation."[15] By interpretation, to be separated from the hour of testing can only mean that the church will have complete immunity from this terrible period of tribulation.

Not only will the church be kept from this period of tribulation, it will also be especially prepared for their entrance into the presence of Jesus Christ. Paul writing to the Corinthians explains:

> Behold, I tell you a mystery; we will not all sleep, but we will all be changed, in a moment, in the twinkling of an eye, at the last trumpet; for the trumpet will sound, and the dead will be raised imperishable, and we will be changed. (1 Corinthians 15:51-52)

Paul states that at the rapture event, the believer's body will be changed in order to inhabit the eternal reward of a heavenly home. He goes on to elaborate that in order to inhabit heaven the believer's human body must be changed so that it is imperishable.

> For this perishable must put on the imperishable, and this mortal must put on immortality. (1 Corinthians 15:53)

And then he declares the ultimate victory for the believer:

> But when this perishable will have put on the imperishable, and this mortal will have put on immortality, then will come about the saying that is written, "Death is swallowed up in victory. O death, where is your victory? O death, where is your sting?" (1 Corinthians 15:54-55)

---

[15] Robertson, A. T. (1934) *A Grammar of the Greek New Testament in the Light of Historical Research*, Nashville, TN: Broadman, p. 597

THE TRIBULATION

As already indicated, this period of human history is the conclusion of the age of Israel. It is explained by theologians as the final week of Daniel's 70 weeks prophecy (Daniel 9). Jeremiah described it as "the time of Jacob's distress" (Jeremiah 30:7). Moses had previously warned Israel of tribulation if they failed to honor their covenants with God (Deuteronomy 4:23-31). The reason for this time frame was determined by God as a period of judgment upon His unfaithful people, Israel. Dr. Chafer explains further that this tribulation period:

> Is the completion of a sequence of predicted years, all of which should intervene between the plucking of Israel off the land, which occurred at the time of the Babylonian captivity, and the final return of that people to their land in the full realization of their covenanted blessings under Messiah's reign.[16]

The "sequence of predicted years" was relayed by the angel Gabriel to Daniel:

> Seventy weeks have been decreed for your people and your holy city, to finish the transgression, to make an end of sin, to make atonement for iniquity, to bring in everlasting righteousness, to seal up vision and prophecy and to anoint the most holy place. (Daniel 9:24)

This period of tribulation, also called the "Great Tribulation,"[17] will last 7 years. W.E. Vine writes that:

> It indicates a definite period spoken of by the Lord in Matt. 24:21, 29; Mark 13:19, 24, where the time is mentioned as preceding His second advent, and as a period in which the Jewish nation, restored to Palestine in unbelief by gentile instrumentality, will suffer an unprecedented outburst of fury... [18]

---

[16] Chafer, 4.364
[17] Matthew 24:21; Revelation 7:14
[18] Vine, *Expository Dictionary,* 2:643

It is important to note that Israel, the Jewish nation today, is a nation still in unbelief of Jesus Christ their Messiah.

The essentials elements of the tribulation are:

1. The cruel reign of the "beast out of the sea" (Rev. 13:1), who, at the beginning of the three and a half years, will break his covenant with the Jews (by virtue of which they will have re-established the temple worship, Dan. 9:27), and show himself in the temple, demanding that he be worshipped as God (Mt. 24:15; 2 Thess. 2:4).

2. The active interposition of Satan "having great wrath" (Rev. 12:12), who gives his power to the Beast (Rev. 13:4, 5).

3. The unprecedented activity of demons (Rev. 9:2, 11).[19]

4. Judgment upon the world. The three series of judgments describe these judgments (seals, Rev. 6; trumpets, Rev. 8-9; bowls, Rev. 16);

5. Persecution of Israel (Matt. 24:9; 22; Rev. 12:17).

6. Salvation of multitudes (Rev. 7).

7. Rise of dominion of Antichrist (2 Thess. 2; Rev. 13).[20]

During this time there will be great satanic adversity to the Lord God and His people. This will be led by a triumvirate of evil: the great red dragon (Satan, Revelation 12:3, 9), the Beast (the Antichrist, the head of the Gentile powers), and the False Prophet, who encourages the worship of the Beast. Pentecost describes this as "the unholy trinity, or the trinity of hell"[21] because of its attempts to replicate the Triune Godhead.

Jesus indicated the intensity of this period of tribulation:

> Unless those days had been cut short, no life would have

---

[19] Points 1 – 3 are from: Scofield, p. 1337, *note* 1

[20] Points 4 – 7 are from: Ryrie, *Ryrie Study Bible*, p. 2076

[21] Pentecost, p. 337

been saved; but for the sake of the elect those days will be cut short. (Matthew 24:22)

The culminating event of this period will be the battle of Armageddon (Revelation 19:17-21). There the army of the Lord Jesus Christ will defeat those who came to make war against Him.

THE SECOND COMING OF JESUS CHRIST

Revelation 19:11-16 describes the return of Jesus Christ to the earth in fulfillment of prophecy (Zechariah 14:4; Matthew 24: 29-31; 25: 31). He returns as the all powerful and victorious One, leading a heavenly army against the forces of evil and wiping out the rebellion instigated by the triumvirate of evil. The Beast and False Prophet are thrown into the Lake of Fire and Satan is bound by chain in the "abyss" (Revelation 20:1-3), there he is to remain for the next 1000 years, during which time the Lord Jesus Christ will establish His promised Millennial Kingdom.

THE MILLENNIAL KINGDOM

The focal point of Jesus Christ's return to earth will be the fulfillment of all the *unconditional* elements of the covenants with His people, Israel, including setting up His kingdom reign on earth. Geisler accurately defines this administration:

> The messianic kingdom is a visible, earthly, political kingdom promised to Israel in which Christ, her Messiah, will reign from a throne in Jerusalem over the whole earth, with His apostles and other disciples serving Him. This rule will bring both peace and justice for all people and will last "a thousand years."[22]

The specific unconditional elements of the covenants that will be fulfilled are:

---

[22] Geisler, 4.461

1. The promise of a land, a seed (originating from Abraham), and to be made a blessing to all the nations – these are contained in the Abrahamic covenant, Genesis 12:1-7. Concerning this, Pentecost states:

   > These words *land* and *seed*, together with the word *blessing*, summarize the essential features of the eschatological portion of the covenant [emphasis his].[23]

2. The promise of regathering Israel to their promised land – this is detailed in the Palestinian covenant, Deuteronomy 30:1-10.

3. The promise of an everlasting king, a throne and a royal house from the lineage of David – these are contained in the Davidic covenant, 2 Samuel 7:12-16.

4. The promise of a new heart and the forgiveness of sin – these unconditional elements were relayed by the prophets Isaiah, Ezekiel and specifically, Jeremiah 31:31-34.

The prophet Ezekiel's summation of these unconditional elements of the covenants which God made with His people, Israel, outlines the purpose of the Millennial reign of Jesus Christ, the Messiah. It would be beneficial to include them here:

> Again the word of the Lord came to me, saying, "As for you, son of man, take a stick for yourself and write on it: 'For Judah and for the children of Israel, his companions.' Then take another stick and write on it, 'For Joseph, the stick of Ephraim, and for all the house of Israel, his companions.' Then join them one to another for yourself into one stick, and they will become one in your hand.
>
> "And when the children of your people speak to you, saying, 'Will you not show us what you mean by these?'—say to them, 'Thus says the Lord God: "Surely I will take the stick of Joseph, which is in the hand of Ephraim, and the tribes of Israel, his companions; and

---

[23] Pentecost, p.84

I will join them with it, with the stick of Judah, and make them one stick, and they will be one in My hand." ' And the sticks on which you write will be in your hand before their eyes.

"Then say to them, 'Thus says the Lord God: "Surely I will take the children of Israel from among the nations, wherever they have gone, and will gather them from every side and bring them into their own land; and I will make them one nation in the land, on the mountains of Israel; and one king shall be king over them all; they shall no longer be two nations, nor shall they ever be divided into two kingdoms again. They shall not defile themselves anymore with their idols, nor with their detestable things, nor with any of their transgressions; but I will deliver them from all their dwelling places in which they have sinned, and will cleanse them. Then they shall be My people, and I will be their God.

"David My servant shall be king over them, and they shall all have one shepherd; they shall also walk in My judgments and observe My statutes, and do them. Then they shall dwell in the land that I have given to Jacob My servant, where your fathers dwelt; and they shall dwell there, they, their children, and their children's children, forever; and My servant David shall be their prince forever. Moreover I will make a covenant of peace with them, and it shall be an everlasting covenant with them; I will establish them and multiply them, and I will set My sanctuary in their midst forevermore. My tabernacle also shall be with them; indeed I will be their God, and they shall be My people. The nations also will know that I, the Lord, sanctify Israel, when My sanctuary is in their midst forevermore." ' " (Ezekiel 37:15-28 NKJV)

A final note: according to Ezekiel 37:21, above, God states that He will gather together the nation of Israel into the land. It will not be, as is presently the case, a Gentile contrived restoration of Jews into the land. Man cannot and will not bring in the end of the age; the sovereign God of the universe will accomplish all that He promises.

THE END OF THE KINGDOM AGE

At the end of the 1000 year reign of Jesus Christ, Satan will be released from the abyss. The Apostle John provides the details of the events which follow in the book of Revelation:

> When the thousand years are completed, Satan will be released from his prison, and will come out to deceive the nations which are in the four corners of the earth, Gog and Magog, to gather them together for the war; the number of them is like the sand of the seashore. And they came up on the broad plain of the earth and surrounded the camp of the saints and the beloved city, and fire came down from heaven and devoured them. (Revelation 20:7-9)

An army will assemble from the four corners of the earth (i.e. all over the world), numbering as the sand of the sea. Where do all these people come from in a thousand year period? Strauss answers this question:

> If one wonders where these masses of people come from, he need only be reminded that the millennium will be the time of earth's greatest population explosion, because the curse will be removed from the physical earth, thereby yielding its greatest food production. Likewise disease will be eliminated.[24]

It is interesting to note, that despite the physical presence of Jesus Christ reigning on earth, there will still be those who will provoke an opposition to the Almighty One. This demonstrates that even

---

[24] Strauss, Lehman (1985) *The Book of the Revelation*, Neptune, NJ: Loizeaux Brothers, p.339

while living in perfect environmental conditions (for there could be no more perfect reign than that of Jesus Christ's) the hearts and minds of men will still have the inclination to turn to evil. Alford wrote concerning this:

> There will be nations on earth besides the saints reigning with Christ, who during the binding of Satan have been quiet and willing subjects of the Kingdom, but who on his [Satan] being let loose are again subjected to his temptations, which stir them into rebellion against God.[25]

The Apostle John notes that this army will be defeated by fire raining down from the heavens and devouring them.

THE JUDGMENTS

There are two major judgments described in John's revelation occurring at the end of the Millennium – Satan and the Great White Throne judgment.

Of Satan

> And the devil who deceived them was thrown into the lake of fire and brimstone, where the beast and the false prophet are also; and they will be tormented day and night forever and ever. (Revelation 20:10)

This is the culmination of the career of God's arch enemy - Satan, Lucifer, the devil. Victory over the evil one had been predicted as far back as Genesis 3:15, when Satan deceived the woman in the Garden of Eden.

The triumvirate of evil (Satan, the beast and the false prophet) are to suffer forever in the Lake of Fire, prepared for the devil and his angels (Matthew 25:41). And thus will God end the matter of evil in His creation. The eternal state to come will be devoid of all evil and

---

[25] Alford, Henry (1878) *The Greek Testament*, Boston, MA: Lee and Shepard Publishers, 4.733

the temptation to sin. All will live in the righteousness and eternal fellowship of Jesus Christ.

One final note concerning evil: no other earthly religion deals with the subject of evil as does Christianity. They offer no final solution to the matter of evil as the God of the Bible does.

The Great White Throne Judgment – Revelation 20:11-15

In John's vision of this final judgment, he sees the entire world population of unbelievers standing before this great white throne of the Supreme Ruler of the universe. There are books opened, out of which the individuals works have been recorded, good deeds and evil deeds. From these books their works are judged to determine if they are sufficient to merit salvation. Their eternal fate rests upon whether their names are found in the book of life, which entry is based solely upon whether they had believed in Jesus Christ (John 3:16, 36). However, the righteous have already been judged of their works,[26] so it is a certainty that these before the white throne of God will not be found in the book of life. They will be cast into the lake of fire for all eternity.

Thus ends human history as we know it. The Apostle Paul wrote concerning the event which would mark the end of days:

> Then comes the end, when He hands over the kingdom to the God and Father, when He has abolished all rule and all authority and power. For He must reign until He has put all His enemies under His feet. The last enemy that will be abolished is death. (1 Corinthians 15:24-26)

All subversive human and supernatural powers are defeated (Revelation 20:9-10) and the last enemy, death, will be thrown into the Lake of Fire as recorded in Revelation 20:14.

---

[26] Christians - At the return of Christ for His church (1 Corinthians 4:5; 2 Timothy 4:8); Israel - At the end of the Tribulation (Revelation 20:4ff).

The Eternal State

What comes next in God's end time program is known as the Eternal State. John's outlines this in Revelation 21:1-22:5:

1. The new heaven and new earth, not a restored earth,[27] because it has "passed away," 21:1

2. The new city of Jerusalem, descending from out of heaven, 21:2

3. The characteristics of the eternal state: no more death, mourning, crying, pain, 21:4

4. The description of the New Jerusalem, 21:9-23

5. The glorious majesty of the New Jerusalem, 21:24-22:5

Chafer in noting that there will only be two spheres of existence in eternity, hell and heaven, states that:

> However, in many Bible passages (cf. Isa. 65:17; 66:22; Heb. 1:10-12; 2 Pet. 3:10-14; Rev. 20:11; 21:1-4) it is declared that there will be a new earth as well as a new heaven, and that the earthly people, Israel, go on forever in the glorified earth that is to be (cf. Isa. 66:22; Jer. 31:36-37), and that the Davidic kingdom which is earthly and to be centered in Jerusalem will continue forever and ever (cf. Isa. 9:6-7; Dan. 7:14; Luke 1:31-33; Rev. 11:15). [28]

Scripture maintains that the future of Israel will be earthly -related to the possession of the Promised Land; while the church of Jesus Christ has a heavenly destiny (John 14:2-3; Ephesians 2:6; Hebrews 12:22-24). Vine writes "for the position, establishment and destiny of the Church are heavenly. It constitutes 'the Church of the firstborn who are enrolled in heaven' " [quoting Heb. 12:23].[29]

The new heavens will include the heavenly Jerusalem that descends

---

[27] Peter describes the destruction of the earth in 2 Peter 3:7-13.

[28] Chafer, 4.419

[29] Vine, *Collected Writings*, 5.224

from heaven and is suspended over the earth, as described in Revelation 21:2, prepared for a bride. It is this same heavenly Jerusalem mentioned by the writer of Hebrews:

> But you have come to Mount Zion and to the city of the living God, the heavenly Jerusalem, and to myriads of angels. (Hebrews 12:22)

Chafer comments on this passage:

> It will be seen that this description articulates with the description of the city given in Revelation 21:10-22:7. God will be there, Christ will be there, the angels will be there, the Church will be there, and the "spirits of just men made perfect" – according to Hebrews – and the twelve tribes of Israel – according to revelation – will be there. [30]

CONCLUSION

It is important to state at the conclusion of this brief outline of the End Times, that the literal-grammatical method of interpretation was employed. The student of the Word who spiritualizes the meaning of Scripture or utilizes the allegorical method of interpretation will skew his world-life view, and misunderstand the directives which God has for the church today as well as in the future. For example, if one were to spiritualize the promises made to Israel so that they will realize their fulfillment by the Church today, then the goal of the Church (as is the aim of many denominations) is to work in order to bring about the kingdom promised to Israel. However, this violates the plain meaning of Scripture that states that Jesus Christ will institute His kingdom (Revelation 20:4-6), and the eternal state (Revelation 21:1-22:5).

Donald Bloesch describes this eschatological view which is within Catholicism:

> He [Johannes Metz] sees the future that the church hopes

---

[30] Chafer, 4.419

for "emerging" and "arising" in the here and now. In place of an otherworldly eschatology he proposes "a creative and militant eschatology" which seeks the overthrow of oppressive power structures in society. The this-worldly character of his theology of hope is apparent in his statement:

"Our eschatological expectation does not look for the heavenly-earthly Jerusalem as that ready-made and existing, promised city of God. This heavenly city does not lie ahead of us as a distant and hidden goal, which only needs to be revealed. The eschatological City of God is now coming into existence, for out hopeful approach builds this city. We are workers building this future, and not just interpreters of this future. The power of God's promises for the future moves us to form this world into the eschatological city of God." [31]

Our interpretation of the end times is not meant to instruct the church as to what it should be doing today; these directives have been clearly set down in the New Testament Epistles. There is no denying that the writers of the Epistles instruct the church to be active as a witness to our culture today. Nevertheless, the correct interpretation of the end times is to demonstrate that God's plan for the ages has indeed a beginning as well as an ending, of which He and He alone has supreme control over the events leading up to the eternal state.

---

[31] Metz, Johannes (1969) *Theology of the World*, New York, NY: Herder & Herder, pp. 94-95, quoted in: Bloesch, Donald G. (2001) *Essentials of Evangelical Theology*, Peabody, MA: Prince Press, 2.176-177

CHAPTER CHECK

1. Define what a "dispensation" is, and how they help in the understanding of God's plan for the ages.

2. What does it mean that the Church is an intercalary period?

3. When does the Rapture of the Church occur?

4. Explain what the Tribulation entails.

5. What will Jesus Christ do at His second coming?

6. What unconditional covenantal promises will be fulfilled in the Millennial Kingdom?

7. Explain what will happen to Satan during the end times.

8. In what way does ones interpretation of Bible prophecy determine their world view?

* * * * * * * *

PART II SUMMARY

The intent of Part II was not to provide an exhaustive or comprehensive presentation of the basic doctrines of the Christian faith. Instead the objective was to provide a unified basis for the undeniable truths that are pertinent to the truth statements of the Christian faith. From this base, the church will be enabled and empowered by the Holy Spirit to project a consistent and cohesive witness of Jesus Christ, our Lord and Savior before an unbelieving world. To believe that this could be accomplished by a variety of "Christian" sects who fail to maintain the "one faith" of Ephesians 4:5, is in effect an open offense to the intended meaning of God's Word. There must be unity in the Body of Christ, not merely lip service to our Lord and His Word, but a unity of doctrine that rules *all* believers in Jesus Christ.

Part III:

THE EXHIBITION OF THE CHRISTIAN FAITH

❧ 11 ❧

THE DYNAMICS OF A
PURIFIED LIFE, PART I

In the introduction, Dr. Francis Schaeffer was quoted with regard to his suggested course of action for the church so that it would become a vibrant witness within our culture today. His statement repeated:

> As the bride of Christ, the church is to keep itself pure and faithful. And this involves two principles which seem at first to work against each other: (1) the principle of the practice of the purity of the visible church in regard to doctrine and life; and (2) the principle of the practice of an observable love and oneness among *all* true Christians regardless of who and where they are. [emphasis his][1]

The first principle was addressed in Part II. The need for a unified basis of belief with its foundation firmly rooted in the authoritative Word provides the only means by which the church is able to present a cohesive witness before the world. Without this, the task before believers, individually and collectively, is destined to fall short. Yet, it is possible for the church to succeed in its objective. But it would require that believers live an exemplary life in harmony with doctrine. However, the practice of our faith must never be attempted in our own strength; it must be undertaken in the power of the Holy Spirit.

---

[1] Schaeffer, 4.115

This second principle, the dynamics that will enable the believer in his practice of an observable love and oneness, will be examined in this chapter and the next chapter. If the church of Jesus Christ were to demonstrate true love and unity in a coordinated manner, their witness of Christ would have great impact upon a fallen world. The successful implementation of these principles requires individual believers to learn and employ the dynamics for the Christian life. They are almost all but forgotten within Christianity today, having been replaced with emotional activities designed to arouse a feeling of self-satisfaction. Instead believers should develop an earnest desire to serve Jesus Christ within the boundaries of His written Word and by the empowerment of the Holy Spirit. Much of the activities in Christian circles today are self-serving and an attempt to substitute the evil within the entertainment world by providing "Christian" entertainment alternatives. Do not be confused by this criticism, there is absolutely nothing wrong or sinful with enjoying and participating in entertainment activities (provided they do not violate Scriptural tenets). It is the state of the believer's mind that is in question here. It is a matter of putting the priorities of the believer's life into their proper Biblical perspective.

By way of illustrating this point, most people's priorities of life could be represented by the pie chart in Figure 1. The priorities of a person prior to having trusted in Christ as their Savior would look like this:

LIFE'S PRIORITIES

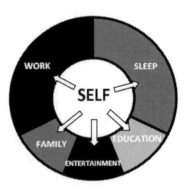

FIG. 1

It is obvious that much of the average person's time is spent in work related activities and sleeping, leaving very little time for the other involvements in their lives: family, entertainment, etc. The center of their life dictates what the priority is for each hour of the day, based upon self interests and desires.

When a person accepts Christ as his Savior, what they tend to do is to find a place in their priorities to fit Jesus or church activities. Their chart might look like this:

LIFE'S PRIORITIES

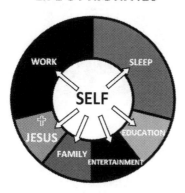

FIG. 2

He now has found a way to add Jesus to his life in the same manner in which one might add a social club or a political endeavor to their priorities in life. This is a wholly un-Scriptural approach and is the result of a flawed evangelization technique. When a person claims Christ as his Savior, he does so primarily because it is the right thing to do before his Creator, but also he desires to have his life transformed from the pollution of this world to a righteous life of serving God. It doesn't mean that he necessarily gives up time spent with family or in the field of his livelihood. It means that there is a new center to his life, which permeates all of his activities of life. This new life in Christ may well weed out some things that are violations of God's holy standards, but the new believer must understand that he now has a new life to live as opposed to the one in which *he* was the center. Instead, all that he does and plans for in life is now directed by his Lord and Savior through prayer and careful study of His Word.

The believer's life chart should look like this:

LIFE'S PRIORITIES

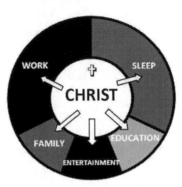

FIG. 3

With Jesus Christ at the center, this realizes the Biblical mandate for the prioritization of the believer's life. This should be the very first principle learned by the new believer in Jesus Christ in order to ensure that he has the proper basis to begin living the purified life.

The next objective is for the believer to understand that there are divine operating assets which are made available for the advancement in the Christian life in order for the believer to reach his Spiritual Growth Potential (SGP). These operating principles are the dynamics of the Christian life, designed to nurture and empower every believer. These principles include: confession of sin; the principle of true spirituality; prayer; and the wealth of promises (these last two will be dealt with in the next chapter).

SIN AND THE BELIEVER

God's divine purpose of providing mankind with the means for salvation from the penalty of sins was so that they could be reconciled to Him and to enjoy fellowship with Him in time and in eternity. The implication of this is far greater than the erroneous belief that

God provides salvation so that man will escape the punishment of hell. Salvation is not simply fire insurance. If this were true, then the subject of the believer's personal sins after salvation would be a moot point. The offer of salvation is a serious matter for the unsaved individual to consider. Therefore, it is critical for the Christian who witnesses the Gospel message to make the issue clear. Accepting Christ as Savior is not an exercise in "covering one's bets" in order to ensure a place in heaven *if* the Gospel and Christ should happen to be true. Accepting Christ as Savior is to truly believe that Christ is who He says He is and that He provided the means by which one can be saved and reconciled with their Creator. Therefore, the one who believes the Gospel of Christ is one who seeks to complete his life as it was originally intended by the Creator – by achieving a moment-by-moment relationship with his heavenly Father.

Sin Defined

Technically, according to W.E. Vine, the word sin in the Greek refers to: "a missing of the mark," and he adds:

> But this etymological meaning is largely lost sight of in the NT. It is the most comprehensive term for moral obliquity [perversity].[2]

Simply put, Chafer states that "sin is that which proves unlike the character of God."[3] In other words, anything which disregards or defies the holy character of God is open rebellion and thus sin.

This is God's universal standard which applies to *all* mankind. It is further described in *Nelson's New Illustrated Bible Dictionary* as:

> Lawlessness (1 John 3:4) or transgression of God's will, either by omitting to do what God's law requires or by doing what it forbids. The transgression can occur in thought (1 John 3:15), word (Matt. 5:22), or deed (Rom. 1:32)…Sin is not represented in the Bible as the absence of good, or as an illusion that stems from our human

---

[2] Vine, *Expository Dictionary,* 2:576
[3] Chafer, 7.287

limitations. Sin is portrayed as a real and positive evil. Sin is more than unwise, inexpedient, calamitous behavior that produces sorrow and distress. It is rebellion against God's law—the standard of righteousness (Ps. 119:160).[4]

The writer of Proverbs describes seven sins which the Lord hates:

> [1] Haughty eyes, [2] a lying tongue, and [3] hands that shed innocent blood, [4] a heart that devises wicked plans, [5] feet that run rapidly to evil, [6] a false witness who utters lies, and [7] one who spreads strife among brothers (Proverbs 6:17-19).

However, any sin in God's eyes is equally sinful, and a violation of His holy standards.

Therefore, since all men are creatures of the Creator, they are expected to live by His standard of holiness. When they "miss the mark" or defy the directives of God, they are rebellious and produce lawlessness which is the expression of sin. It is for this reason man must trust in Jesus Christ, who died on the cross, suffering our penalty and paying the price for the remission of sins – the only means by which man can be reconciled with his Creator.

Do Believers Still Sin?

There is much Scriptural support for the fact that once believers are saved that they will still have struggles with sin and obedience to the divine standards of living. The Apostle John writing to fellow Christians stated:

> If we say that we have no sin, we are deceiving ourselves and the truth is not in us... If we say that we have not sinned, we make Him a liar and His word is not in us. (1 John 1:8, 10)

---

4 Youngblood, R. F. (1997, c1995) *Nelson's New Illustrated Bible Dictionary*: An authoritative one-volume reference work on the Bible with full color illustrations (F. Bruce, Ed.) (electronic ed. of the revised ed. of Nelson's Illustrated Bible Dictionary) Nashville, TN: Thomas Nelson

The Apostle Paul likewise provides instructions to believers that they should "walk in the Spirit, and you will not carry out the desire of the flesh,"[5] and, "be imitators of God."[6] These would be idle words if indeed Christians did not sin. This is not a condoning of sin. It does not mean that a person can be saved with the attitude that he can now live an unrestrained life of open rebellion to God's standards. For those who attempt to will receive discipline of the Lord.[7] The appropriate attitude of the Christian is to be unwavering in living a holy and obedient life.

The Results of Sin in the Believer

There is a two-fold effect of sin in the life of the believer: upon himself and upon his heavenly Father. The believer loses out on precious time of fellowship with God. John writes that:

> If we say that we have fellowship with Him and yet walk in the darkness, we lie and do not practice the truth. (1 John 1:6)

Walking in darkness refers to a Christian who habitually indulges himself in sinning. In just this one verse, John sets the record straight that flagrant sinning is not a part of an acceptable Christian walk. We have no fellowship with God if we engage in sin of any magnitude. We lose out on the moment-by-moment fellowship and as David stated, the joy related to our fellowship with the Lord.[8]

Not only is there an effect upon the believer, God is also affected by the believer's sin. He is unable to enjoy the desired fellowship with His child, and the glory due Him is not realized. Paul speaks of this broken relationship in Ephesians 4:30 the context illustrates that the Holy Spirit is said to be grieved by the believer's sin. The believer is

---

[5] Galatians 5:16

[6] Ephesians 5:1

[7] See Hebrews 12:6-7, the exact type of discipline from the Lord is not clearly spoken of, but John states that "there is a sin leading to death," (1 John 5:16) and some believers who misused the communion table were sickened and died (1 Corinthians 11:27-31).

[8] Psalm 51:12

commanded not to grieve the Holy Spirit. This simple admonition means "Don't sin, or you will grieve the Holy Spirit, the one in whom you are sealed for the day of redemption." Closely related to this is Paul's command to the Thessalonians: "Do not quench the Spirit."[9] When one quenches their thirst, the thirst is gone. So it happens when the Spirit is quenched, He is gone, that is His filling and empowerment. This is why Paul commands that the believer be consistently "filled with the Spirit."[10]

Sin causes the believer to grieve the Spirit and consequently to lose the filling of the Holy Spirit, which empowers the believer in the practice of his faith and makes it possible for him to have meaningful fellowship with his Lord.

Preventative Measures

That the believer should refrain from personal sin is clearly stated in Scripture. However, it is easier said than done. And yet preventative measures have been provided that every believer should employ in their daily lives in order to avoid sin.

First and foremost, the believer should endeavor to become established in the knowledge of God's Word. David stated his strategy regarding this very issue:

> Your word I have treasured in my heart, that I may not sin against You. (Psalm 119:11)

There is power in knowing God and understanding His demands of righteous living. The child of God will know the difference between the path of righteous living and sinful life styles when he demonstrates a sincere and active pursuit of the knowledge of God's Word. There is no substitute for the knowledge and application of God's Word in order for the believer to successfully imitate Christ and to have a victorious walk of faith. Dr. Chafer echoes this:

> There is little hope for victory in daily life on the part of

---

[9] 1 Thessalonians 5:19
[10] Ephesians 5:18

those believers who, being ignorant of the Word of God, do not know the nature of their conflict or the deliverance God has provided.[11]

Second, the believer should be aware of the intercessory work of Christ upon his behalf. Paul writes in Romans 8:34 that Christ is presently at the right hand of God and intercedes for us. Why would He be doing this for us? Because whenever a Christian sins, Satan, the accuser of the brethren, is making accusations before the throne of God, day and night.[12] This is corroborated by the writer of the book of Hebrews stating that He always lives to make intercession for us.[13]

This means that the believer must do something about his personal sins. Since sin is inevitable in the life of the believer, he should therefore be ever vigilant. Upon the occasion of sin, he must pray for power to overcome temptation. And if he should fall into sin, he must confess the sin in order to seek cleansing from the Father through the intercessory ministry of Christ. John gives the instruction for receiving cleansing:

> If we confess our sins, He is faithful and righteous to forgive us our sins and to cleanse us from all unrighteousness. (1 John 1:9)

Unfortunately, there is much confusion over this principle within Christianity today. It should be noted that this is not a license for the believer to sin, that is, making it easy to seek out forgiveness and cleansing simply to go back and sin some more. John instructs us to seek forgiveness and cleansing so that we will be able to walk in the light and be empowered and usable for the purpose which God has called us.

Also, our confession of sins should take place immediately after the occasion of sin. This would imply that our walk with the Lord should be so close to our moment-by-moment experiences that we know right away that we have stepped out of the boundaries of

---

[11] Chafer, 2.333
[12] Revelation 12:10
[13] Hebrews 7:25

righteous living. The believer who waits until he lies down to sleep at night to confess his sins takes the chance of losing a whole day of fellowship and service for his Lord. Van Ryn emphasizes that the believer should keep short accounts with God:

> The believer should daily confess every sin to God – keep short accounts with Him – so that he may have the Father's forgiveness and the cleansing application of the truth of God, thus keeping him in communion with God.[14]

This is not to say that we might have to contemplate certain actions, words or thoughts in order to recognize or admit their sinfulness. In situations like these, the believer should prayerfully ask for guidance and search God's Word. It is just such determination that will hasten the believer to a victorious life.

The third preventative measure has been mentioned previously: the filling of the Holy Spirit. It is set forth in Paul's command to the believer in Ephesians 5:18:

> And do not get drunk with wine, for that is dissipation [indulgence], but be filled with the Spirit.

Dr. Wuest comments on this verse:

> The interpretation is, "Be constantly, moment by moment, being controlled by the Spirit."[15]

The analogy which Paul sets up is relatively simple. Just as too much wine will control the thinking and motor skills of an individual, the believer filled with the Holy Spirit is under His controlling influence. Dr. Wuest has a pertinent explanation:

> We must not think of the Holy Spirit filling our hearts as water fills a bottle, or air, a vacuum, or a bushel of oats, an empty basket. The heart of a Christian is not a receptacle to be emptied in order that the Holy Spirit might fill it. The Holy Spirit is not a substance to fill an empty

---

[14] Van Ryn, August (1948) *The Epistles of John*, New York, NY: Loizeaux Brothers, p.41

[15] Wuest, Vol. I, "Ephesians and Colossians," p. 128

receptacle. He is a Person to control another person, the believer. He does not fill a Christian's life with Himself. He controls that person.[16]

Since this command is a continuous action, it implies that the believer may *not* always be filled with the Holy Spirit. This means that when there is unconfessed sin in the life of the believer, the controlling influence of the Spirit is not present. This should not be confused with the doctrine of the indwelling of the Holy Spirit. His indwelling ministry never departs from the believer, for the believer is sealed by the Holy Spirit unto the day of redemption.[17]

Prompt confession of sin is the identifying mark of an obedient believer, one who is controlled by the Holy Spirit, who has the capacity for a meaningful relationship with his Lord, one who has the ability to fulfill the purpose which God has for his life. This is what is meant by living a victorious moment-by-moment Christian life. Again, Dr. Wuest's comment:

> The control which the Spirit exerts over the believer is dependent upon the believer's active and correct adjustment to the Spirit…There must be an ever present conscious dependence upon and definite subjection to the Holy Spirit, a constant yielding to His ministry and leaning upon Him for guidance and power, if He is to control the believer *in the most efficient manner and with the largest and best results…* One of the reasons why the Holy Spirit has so little control over many Christians is because they think He works automatically in their hearts [emphasis his].[18]

This "correct adjustment to the Spirit" requires that the believer be willing and determined to serve his Lord by being obedient to the directives contained in His Word.

---

[16] Wuest, Vol. III, "Untranslatable Riches," p. 104

[17] Ephesians 4:30 - The day of redemption is the final aspect of the Christian life, when the believer reaches his eternal reward either at death or when the Rapture of the church occurs.

[18] Wuest, Vol. III, "Untranslatable Riches," p. 105-106

TRUE SPIRITUALITY

True spirituality is that quality of life in the child of God which satisfies and glorifies the Father.[19]

The subject of true spirituality as it pertains to the believer is to be viewed from two perspectives: 1) The status of the believer concerning his relationship with the Holy Spirit, and 2) the outworking of the Holy Spirit in the believer's life which counteracts evil and produces divine good.

Considering both of these aspects, Chafer explains spirituality in this manner:

> As related to man, spirituality represents that manner of life which is wrought in (not by) the believer by the unhindered, indwelling Spirit of God (Romans 8:4).[20]

Elsewhere he writes that:

> Spirituality contemplates two achievements, namely, overcoming evil and promoting that which is good in the believer's life and experience. The one is negative – a disannulling of evil, the other is positive – a realization of the supernatural qualities and accomplishments which belong to a superhuman manner of life.[21]

To misunderstand or to minimize this dynamic of the Christian life is to short circuit the productive life of the believer.

The Believer's Status

As mentioned in the last section, the Biblical status of the believer ought ideally to be rightly adjusted to the Holy Spirit. That is, the believer is to be free of unconfessed sin and with the determination and willingness to serve his Lord. However, this is not always the case

---

[19] Chafer, Lewis Sperry (1967) *He That Is Spiritual,* Grand Rapids, MI: Zondervan, p.7

[20] Chafer, *Systematic Theology,* 7.292

[21] Chafer, *Systematic Theology,* 6.177

for all believers. The Apostle Paul explains that there are believers who are not spiritual. He declares these believers to be "carnal."

> And I, brethren, could not speak to you as to spiritual people but as to carnal, as to babes in Christ. (1 Corinthians 3:1 NKJV)

A "carnal" believer literally means one whose life is characterized by fleshly self desires. These believers are not interested in the study of God's Word nor are they concerned with developing a Christ centered life. They typically synthesize the lifestyles of the world with a thin self-styled veneer of Christianity. The trend today with liberal Christians is to abandon the need of dealing with personal sin for fear that it would damage the individual's self-esteem.[22] This is the type of compromise which engenders doctrinal divisions.

The believer is not to be carnally minded – he is to be spiritual. He is to desire the pure milk of the Word in order to grow up and reach his spiritual growth potential.[23] And in order to achieve the necessary growth, his status moment-by-moment should be that of being "spiritual." He is to keep short accounts with God concerning sin, and maintain the proper attitude of being actively ready to serve his Lord.

This is the first step of true spirituality. The believer must achieve this status and consistently endeavor to sustain this right adjustment to the Holy Spirit if he is to fulfill the next aspect of spirituality.

The Spirit Driven Believer

The second aspect of spirituality is the operation of the Holy Spirit in the life of the believer. Under the guidance of the Holy Spirit, the believer is enabled in his understanding of God's Word, empowered for the production of divine good, and, additionally, provision is made available for spiritual warfare. These manifestations of the

---

[22] Note the absence of the subject of sin in the popular book by Rick Warren, *The Purpose Driven Life*, Grand Rapids, MI: Zondervan Publishing House, 2002.
[23] 1 Peter 2:2

Spirit driven believer are realized internally and externally. They include: illumination of Scripture; fruit of the Spirit; the power to overcome evil; the believer's spiritual armor; and the believer's walk of faith.

1) Illumination of Scripture

Many believers have rightfully asked the question: "What Christian service should I become involved in?" Dr. Francis Schaeffer exposes the flawed viewpoint of some in Christianity today:

> Often, after a person is born again and asks, "What shall I do next?" he is given a list of things, usually of a limited nature, and primarily negative. Often he is given the idea that if he does not do this series of things (whatever this series of things happens to be in the particular country and location and at the time he happens to live), he will be spiritual. This is not so.[24]

Schaeffer's observation is right. Spirituality is not refraining from a series of taboos, nor is it following a pattern of behavior that is dictated apart from God's Word. Paul stated that the problem of carnality with the Corinthians was that they were not able to take in solid food. This solid food is the deep truths of God's Word, the foundations of our faith.

Concerning the origins of this foundation Paul wrote:

> For no man can lay a foundation other than the one which is laid, which is Jesus Christ. (1 Corinthians 3:11)

So the believer must always begin with Scripture as his guide for faith and the practice of his faith. There is no substitute for the authoritative directing of the Christian's life. It is therefore essential for spiritual growth that the believer be diligent in studying God's Word. Dr. Wuest comments that:

> The Christian who does not maintain a real interest in and hunger for the Word of God, and satisfy both by a constant study of that Word, is not co-operating with the Spirit, and is not giving the Spirit an opportunity to work

---

[24] Schaeffer, 3.201

in his life and cause him to grow in the Christian graces. The Spirit works through the Word of God that we have stored in our hearts, and not apart from it.[25]

Since the Spirit works through the believer based on his knowledge of the Word, it is essential for the believer to understand God's Word in order to make the proper application of God's Word in his life. And this is accomplished through the illuminating work of the Holy Spirit. The Apostle Paul detailed this ministry of the Spirit:

> Now we have received, not the spirit of the world, but the Spirit who is from God, so that we may know the things freely given to us by God, which things we also speak, not in words taught by human wisdom, but in those taught by the Spirit, combining spiritual thoughts with spiritual words. (1 Corinthians 2:12-13)

It is through the power of the indwelling Holy Spirit that provides comprehension of God's Word to *all* the saints.[26] It is not provided to just a select group of Christians. It is not given only to those who have an elevated IQ. These truths are for *all of the saints*; to help *all* in reaching their spiritual growth potential. This knowledge is not just to be learned in the seminaries and then withheld from the man in the pew thinking that they are too dim to understand. Yet this is what has transpired over the past century and has directly contributed to the weakening of the witness of Christianity in our culture today. There is no substitute for the knowledge of God's Word in the directing of the believer's life in order for him to attain the end purpose which God has for him.

Dr. Chafer explains the necessity of this illuminating ministry of the Holy Spirit:

> Were it not for this divine resource and sufficiency, the superhuman manner of life now expected from each believer would be an impossible and, therefore, an inconsistent requisition.[27]

---

[25] Wuest, "Untranslatable Riches," p. 113

[26] Ephesians 3:18

[27] Chafer, *Systematic Theology*, 1.109

2) The Fruit of the Spirit

One of the great internal works of the Holy Spirit is His transforming ministry that is designed to make the believer more like the Son of God. As explained by the Apostle Paul in Galatians 5:17, this internal makeover of the believer is to counteract the conflict of fleshly desires with the leading of the Spirit:

> For the flesh sets its desire against the Spirit, and the Spirit against the flesh; for these are in opposition to one another, so that you may not do the things that you please.

In verses 19 through 21 Paul identifies these sins of the flesh:

> Now the deeds of the flesh are evident, which are: immorality, impurity, sensuality, idolatry, sorcery, enmities, strife, jealousy, outbursts of anger, disputes, dissensions, factions, envying, drunkenness, carousing, and things like these...

In naming these deeds, Paul is attempting to persuade believers to confront and eradicate these evil qualities, reminding them that those whose lives are characterized by these deeds will not partake of the joys of God's kingdom. He then presents a list of godly qualities which can only be realized by the in-working of the Holy Spirit in order to counteract the deeds of the flesh. He describes these qualities in verses 22 and 23 as the fruit of the Spirit:

> But the fruit of the Spirit is love, joy, peace, patience, kindness, goodness, faithfulness, gentleness, self-control; against such things there is no law.

The first point to note is that these nine qualities are called the fruit, singular, not fruits, of the Spirit. Dr. Ryrie comments on this point:

> The fact that these are the fruit, not fruits, of the Spirit reminds us that all nine must be present at the same time, completely integrated and acting on each other and producing a balanced, Spirit-controlled and fruitful life.[28]

---

[28] Ryrie, C. C. (1970) *Balancing the Christian Life*, Chicago, IL: Moody

It is obvious that these qualities are not miraculously grafted into the believer at the moment of accepting Christ as Savior. These characteristics are to be developed in the Christian by the Holy Spirit, and not by human energy. The Christian must spend time studying God's Word in order to understand these qualities and to recognize them in the examples of Christ and other godly men recorded in Scripture. Then, by yielding to the control of the Spirit, the believer can demonstrate these characteristics before those of whom he comes in contact.

Ryrie states that the manifestation of the fruit of the Spirit in the believer is "genuine Christlikeness."[29] While Chafer comments that:

> Compressed into these nine words [the fruit of the Spirit] we have not only the exact statement as to what Christian character is, but a description as well, of the life that Christ lived while here on earth. It is also a statement of that manner of life which He would have the Christian experience here and now...True Christian character is the *"fruit of the Spirit"*...True Christian character is produced *in* the believer, but not *by* the believer...The Christian may realize *at once* the heavenly virtues of Christ: not by trying; but by a right adjustment to the indwelling Spirit. [emphasis his] [30]

It is the exclusive work of the Holy Spirit *in* the believer producing these Christian qualities so that consequently the believer demonstrates the perfect character of Christ.

3) The Power to Overcome Evil

It is primarily the function of the Holy Spirit working in the believer to produce Christ-like qualities. In so doing, the Spirit provides empowerment for the believer to overcome evil. The evil mentioned here is not just sin and sinful behavior, but anything which is at

---

Press, p. 118
[29] Ryrie, *Balancing the Christian Life*, p. 116
[30] Chafer, *He That Is Spiritual*, p. 44-47

variance with the outworking of the Spirit in the life of the believer. Dr. Chafer states that:

> The Christian experiences an unceasing, simultaneous, threefold conflict – with the world, the flesh, and the devil.[31]

The pressures generated by the world and Satan have previously been discussed. The world attempts to influence the believer by its systems of entertainment, education, industrial and political ideologies which are contrary to the Word of God. The believer who allies himself with the world does so by becoming intimate with unbelievers who give sanction to the evils of this world system. This is not to say that the believer is not to have contact with the unbeliever. It simply means that he is to refrain from aligning himself with these influences of evil, so that he does not think, talk, or act exactly like the unbeliever.

The satanic influence is both overt and subtle. Satan's overt actions are demonstrated by his powerful sway over the entire world, infecting all with his evil manipulations. His subtleness is lulling the world into believing that he is just a fairy tale or the Hollywood incarnation of the horned, red-skinned demon carrying a trident. Christians today have also been deceived by these false concepts of Satan and the reality of his demons. Most do not realize the armies of demons that wreak havoc in every culture of the world.

But the battleground of the flesh is an internal struggle equal to the other conflicts in promoting evil and just as difficult to achieve victory over. The believer must first understand this conflict within – the struggle of the old sin nature with the new man in Christ. Paul recognized this when he wrote:

> Therefore if anyone is in Christ, he is a new creature; the old things passed away; behold, new things have come. (2 Corinthians 5:17)

And in Romans:

---

[31] Chafer, *Systematic Theology*, 6.178

For I know that nothing good dwells in me, that is, in my flesh. (Romans 7:18a)

The Apostle knew of this struggle and was divinely moved to write instructing how to overcome this problem that all believers face. He states in Galatians:

> But I say, walk by the Spirit, and you will not carry out the desire of the flesh. For the flesh sets its desire against the Spirit, and the Spirit against the flesh; for these are in opposition to one another, so that you may not do the things that you please. (Galatians 5:16-17)

Paul commands that the believer is to walk *by means of* the empowering Spirit. We are to align ourselves with the Holy Spirit and yield to His leading. And as we become more knowledgeable in His Word, we will become sensitive to His leading moment-by-moment in order to achieve victory over the flesh. Dr. Wuest concludes:

> Thus, the secret of victory over sin is found, not in attempted obedience to a law that has been abrogated, but in subjection to a divine Person, the Holy Spirit, who at the moment the sinner places his faith in the Lord Jesus, takes up His permanent residence in his being for the purpose of ministering to his spiritual needs.[32]

The believer should be ever vigilant of these three sources of opposition. They generate evil in the forms of enticements and temptations intended to lure the believer into sinful situations, drawing them away from reaching their spiritual growth potential and distracting them from fulfilling the divine design for their lives.

4) The Believer's Spiritual Armor

In Ephesians 6:11-18, the Apostle Paul outlines the believer's divine provision for spiritual warfare. In verse 11 he commands all believers to "Put on the full armor of God, so that you will be able to stand firm against the schemes of the devil." For a correct understanding of this provision of armor is it necessary to accept the Bible's literal

---

[32] Wuest, Vol. I, "Galatians," p.153

assertion that there is indeed an unseen spiritual battle going on all about us. It does no good to minimize or to marginalize this relentless conflict. The believer must become serious to the fact of his surroundings – to recognize that the battle is in his own backyard.

Paul emphasizes that this conflict is not a merely a schoolyard brawl or a wrestling match in verse 12:

> For our struggle is not against flesh and blood, but against the rulers, against the powers, against the world forces of this darkness, against the spiritual forces of wickedness in the heavenly places.

It is a winner-take-all battle, where Satan and his forces desire to ensure that the believer becomes a fatality, by neutralizing him and making him feel at home in Satan's world. Chafer likewise underscores the reality of this battle:

> Following this most impressive declaration as to the nature of the conflict and the superior character of the foe both as to number and strength, it could not be otherwise than that the Apostle would stress again, as he does (verse 13), the necessity of *standing* against this foe in an *evil* day, and, having done all, *to stand*. So, again, he refers to the armor of God which God has provided for those who wage this battle. Every effort is made by the Apostle through the Spirit to alarm the child of God into recognizing the serious position in which he is placed. [emphasis his][33]

Since this conflict has been previously discussed, a consideration of the divine enablement made available for the believer's defense and victory is in order. First, in verse 13, Paul commands that the believer:

> Therefore, take up the full armor of God, so that you will be able to resist in the evil day, and having done everything, to stand firm.

Not only is this a command to be followed, a purpose for this

[33] Chafer, Lewis Sperry (1991) *The Epistle to the Ephesians*, Grand Rapids, MI: Kregel, p. 143

command is given – that the believer would be able to resist the evil one, Satan, and to stand firm and remain faithful to his Lord.

In verse 14, Paul writes that to stand firm entails "girding" the loins with truth. The Greek word to gird literally means "to wrap oneself around, to be wrapped around, spoken in reference to the long flowing garments of the Orientals which were pulled up and knotted at the waist for freedom of movement."[34] This is rich with meaning. In the normal sense, when one girded their garments in the ancient world, he was readying himself for a journey. A soldier would use a belt around his waist (loins) in order to hold his sword. Both concepts are implied here: the believer is to ready himself for the battle by wrapping himself with the truth. Again, there is an emphasis upon the necessity of knowing truth (doctrine). Without the knowledge of truth the believer is weaponless. With this truth wrapped around the believer, he is now equipped with the most vital weapon needed for the unseen battle: the Word of God. This is the believer's sword, his weapon of defense.

The believer is also told in verse 14 to "put on the breastplate of righteousness." The soldier's breastplate protected the vital organs which powered his body for battle. The righteousness Paul refers to is, as Chafer states:

> The imputed righteousness of God which is made unto us, being *in Christ*. No "rags" of human righteousness will serve as a breastplate in this combat. [emphasis his][35]

God's righteousness is what powers us in the spiritual battle. We dare not go into the fight and expect victory by employing our own strength. We must go forth in the manner which God has intended.

Continuing with verse 15:

> And having shod your feet with the preparation of the gospel of peace.

Like the military soldier of today, the feet must be protected. But this

---

[34] Zodhiates, G4024
[35] Chafer, *The Epistle to the Ephesians*, p. 144

implies, as Lenski states, to a "ready, eager courage that is due to the gospel which fills us with the peace of God."[36] This peace with God that we now possess should give us confidence wherever the Lord leads us in life. And this life we live *is* the battlefield.

Paul continues in verse 16:

> In addition to all, taking up the shield of faith with which you will be able to extinguish all the flaming arrows of the evil one.

The soldier of the ancient world would rely upon a shield to fend off his opponent's sword and arrows. In this spiritual battle the believer is to use the shield of faith. Faith in this context refers specifically to "that which is believed, body of faith or belief, doctrine."[37] Again, here is a reference for the need of the believer to know doctrine. The fiery arrows represent the steady stream of temptations which are hurled at the believer who is standing firmly for the cause of Christ. The believer with doctrine will be able to extinguish the temptations by calling to mind Scripture that will subdue the assault. Our example of this technique is the Lord Jesus Christ while He confronted Satan in the wilderness temptations.[38] In each of the assaults by Satan the Lord countered with Scripture to defeat the tempter.

In verse 17, Paul says to "take the helmet of salvation," which is literally from the Greek: the helmet which is salvation.[39] Paul states similarly in 1 Thessalonians 5:8, "having put on the breastplate of faith and love, and as a helmet, the hope of salvation." Here the added word "hope" means "a confident expectation,"[40] and could be translated as: "having put on...a helmet of the confident expectation of salvation." In the passage in Ephesians 6:17, it is more emphatic. Concerning this helmet, Lenski explains its function:

---

[36] Lenski, R.C.H. (2001) *Commentary on the New Testament*, Peabody, MA: Hendrickson, 8.667

[37] Arndt, W., Gingrich, F. W., p. 669 §3

[38] Matthew 4:1-11

[39] Vincent, 3.410

[40] Vine, *Expository Dictionary*, 2.311

That which saves and keeps safe protects the head from a fatal or a disabling blow.[41]

This helmet which *is* salvation is designed to provide the believer with absolute confidence in God's ability to deliver in the midst of the battle. We should never exhibit fear while doing battle for the Lord.

Paul also commands in verse 17 to take "the sword of the Spirit, which is the Word of God." This sword of the Spirit is a metaphor for the Word of God. The writer of Hebrews concurs:

> For the Word of God is living and active and sharper than any two-edged sword, and piercing as far as the division of soul and spirit, of both joints and marrow, and able to judge the thoughts and intentions of the heart. (Hebrews 4:12)

This is the only offensive weapon made available to the believer. Since our battle is not against blood and flesh, it is exactly the weapon that we need in the battle against the minds and hearts of those in our culture who are under the sway of the evil one, Satan. If it is the Spirit's sword (and indeed it is) it is a supreme and indestructible weapon.

Paul does not use the Greek word *logos* (λóγος) for "the word" in Ephesians 6:17 but instead it is *rhema* (ῥῆμα), which emphasizes the *utterance* of a word. The power of verbalizing God's words is what is meant to be conveyed. It is the same Greek word which Jesus used in Matthew 4:4 in answering the devil tempting Him in the wilderness:

> "It is written, 'Man shall not live on bread alone, but on every word that proceeds out of the mouth of God.' "

The believer is to go into the battle armed with the Word of God imbedded in his soul, empowered by the Holy Spirit. The outfitting of his armor may take years of preparation by studying God's Word every day. The soldier of the Armed Forces prepares for

[41] Lenski, 8.673

battle by a rigorous daily routine for months. He is never enlisted, handed a gun and sent off into battle. The believer should likewise prepare by arming himself with the Word; knowing the enemy and understanding the battle plan which God has for the age in which he lives. Then he will have the confidence in verbalizing God's utterances and realize victory.

Will there be victory in every battle? The believer will know defeat when he attempts to witness for Christ and either has no confidence in standing up for his faith or when he realizes that he does not have enough knowledge of the Word to give valid answers when confronted by unbelievers. This is not the time for despair. The believer must be honest in evaluating his weaknesses and return to his training of study and prayer.

In verse 18 Paul speaks to this issue of prayer:

> With all prayer and petition pray at all times in the Spirit, and with this in view, be on the alert with all perseverance and petition for all the saints.

Praying at all times in the Spirit is the picture of the moment-by-moment life of the believer. His life ought to be a conscious existence with his Lord. There are no vacations from the Christian life, and this verse emphasizes this by insisting upon consistent prayer and alertness. The believer must be aware of the battle about him and live a prayerful and watchful life, ever prepared for the conflicts that he is drawn into by the world.

5) The Believer's Walk of Faith

If we are in the midst of a battle, can there be any joy or happiness in the Christian life? Certainly, but the believer must live this life in the divinely prescribed manner – controlled and empowered by the Spirit of God. In this way he is able to reproduce the character of Christ in his life, to reach his spiritual growth potential, and become productive in his walk of faith. This is the external evidence of spirituality.

This productive walk of faith is designated in some Christian circles as: Christian service, the practice of one's faith, religious works, or church work. Some of these activities might well include: teaching Sunday school, singing in the choir, ushering, serving as a deacon, witnessing, etc. What shall be revealed in the study of this aspect of spirituality is that all of these endeavors may be included as genuine facets of spirituality, but *only when* they are accomplished while the believer is empowered by the Holy Spirit.

There are believers who perform Christian activities in their own power. These may willingly or ignorantly regard personal sins as insignificant in their relationship to God and neglect to confess them. In doing so, they are *not* rightly related to the Holy Spirit – they are not controlled by the Spirit. Instead, they grieve the Spirit and restrain the Spirit's control of their lives. They then go about their religious activities with the expectation of pleasing God. They erroneously reason that "if what I do is something godly then the Spirit is working in me." This is a clear picture of carnality which Paul spoke of in 1 Corinthians 3.

The Corinthian believers were not able to understand solid Biblical truth – they were spiritual infants (verse 1). They demonstrated this by their petty jealousies and factions over whose disciples they were (verses 3 -4). In verses 8 and 9 Paul states that we are all fellow workers but we will each receive a reward for our own labors. These labors build upon a foundation of which Christ laid first (verse 11). In verses 12 and 13, Paul compares their labors to the qualities of the materials used in this foundation:

> Now if any man builds on the foundation with gold, silver, precious stones, wood, hay, straw, each man's work will become evident; for the day will show it because it is to be revealed with fire, and the fire itself will test the quality of each man's work.

It is obvious that wood, hay and straw are combustible materials and would be burned up in fire. These labors are worthless in constructing a solid foundation. These are comparative to works performed in the power of the flesh and not in the power of the Holy Spirit.

Paul affirms this in verse 14:

> If any man's work which he has built on it remains, he will receive a reward.

From these labors, the believer will be rewarded because they were accomplished in the power of the Spirit. These rewards constitute the production of divine good and are presented in heaven as Paul mentions in 2 Corinthians 5:10.

This is a Biblical truth so often overlooked and neglected in the teaching of new believers. It does no good to provide a checklist of what a Christian is not to do. For the Christian's walk of faith is not simply the sum total what he *doesn't* do (although there are plenty of admonitions against certain life-styles which have already been pointed out). Nor does it constitute adherence to a prescribed set of doctrines, as Schaeffer states:

> I am not a Bible-believing Christian in the fullest sense simply by believing the right doctrines, but as I live in practice in this supernatural world.[42]

However, the Scripture emphasizes that the walk of faith for the believer is to be *productive* because of his knowledge of God's Word (doctrine) – in order to understand what manner of life he is to live – and exemplified by one who implements God's will by being yielded and empowered by the Holy Spirit.

---

[42] Schaeffer, 3.258

CHAPTER CHECK

1. Describe the proper Biblical perspective of life priorities and why is it important to the believer?

2. What is sin?

3. How does sin affect the believer and God?

4. Is there anything that can help a believer not to sin? What are they?

5. Explain what true spirituality is and how it can be attained and maintained by the believer.

6. How is the believer enabled to produce the fruit of the Spirit?

7. What issues of the world attempt to influence the believer? And why is it important to reject them?

8. Write down each element of Spiritual armor and explain their function.

❧ 12 ❧

THE DYNAMICS OF A
PURIFIED LIFE, PART II

The Believer and Prayer

There have been many books written espousing different standpoints on the subject of prayer. Although well intentioned as they are, they have brought about much confusion concerning this ever important facet of the Christian's life. Prayer is the vital line of communication between the believer and God. It is not very profound to state that the communication between the believer and his Lord must be intelligible and persistent. As with any other point of doctrine, the Scriptures provide sufficient information for the Christian concerning the mechanics of prayer. This section entails a Biblical definition; when to pray; the believer's approach; the order of prayer; the qualifications of prayer; and for whom do we pray.

Prayer Defined

As already stated, prayer is the vital communication link between the believer and God, his heavenly Father. It is "the intercourse of the soul with God, not in contemplation or meditation, but in direct address to him."[1] It is based upon mutual trust, the same as a

---

[1] Easton, M. (1996, c1897) *Easton's Bible Dictionary*, Oak Harbor, WA: Logos Research Systems, Inc.

child's relationship with their father. Scofield simply defines prayer in this way:

> Prayer, therefore, is a child's petition to an all-wise, all-loving, and all-powerful, Father-God.[2]

The first step in attaining an intelligent dialogue with God is for the believer to comprehend the attributes of the heavenly Father which Scofield has outlined – "all-wise, all-loving, and all-powerful." Once the believer fully appreciates the magnificence of his heavenly Father, his prayers should contain certain attitudes which Dr. Hodge describes:

> Therein we manifest or express to Him our reverence, and love for his divine perfection, our gratitude for all his mercies, our penitence for our sins, our hope in his forgiving love, our submission to his authority, our confidence in his care, our desires for his favor, and for the providential and spiritual blessings needed for ourselves and others.[3]

These attitudes of reverence, love, gratitude, repentance, hope, submission, confidence and desire of His blessings should be at the core of the believer's relationship with the heavenly Father. When this is evidenced in the heart and mind of the believer, his communication with God is open and intelligent. Chafer expounds further:

> Prayer is communion with God that has been based on confidence born of the knowledge of God. It is not natural to speak to one who is unknown and unknowable as is the case with the unsaved trying to pray; but when God is recognized and real to the heart, there is definiteness in every form of prayer and then, as at no other time or under no other conditions, the praying soul finds rest.[4]

There is no fear of rejection when the believer prays on sound

---

[2] Scofield, p. 1089, *note* 1
[3] Hodge, 3:692
[4] Chafer, *Systematic Theology,* 6.107-108

Scriptural ground – recognizing the holy character of the Father and establishing the proper attitude towards his heavenly Father.

When Should the Believer Pray?

The Apostle Paul provides the best answer to this question in 1 Thessalonians 5:17: "Pray without ceasing." Unceasing by definition means: without intermission, continually, constantly. This almost sounds like a call to a monastic life of piety. However, the Scriptures are meant to be understood logically. The idea here is that the believer's relationship with his Lord is to be rightly adjusted at all times, so that at each and every moment he is able to offer up prayers of any type and have the assurance that the Father hears and answers. This is the part of the Christian life which most believers don't fully understand. Many do not realize that God is ever present with and within the believer, so that a successful moment-by-moment walk of faith can be realized by this close relationship with his Lord.

Praying without ceasing is not an isolated concept. In his concluding remarks concerning the believer's spiritual armor in Ephesians 6:18, Paul states:

> With all prayer and petition pray at all times in the Spirit, and with this in view, be on the alert with all perseverance and petition for all the saints.

Not only is the believer to position himself defensively with the whole armor of God, but he is to be in constant communication with God concerning his needs and those of all the saints.

In Colossians 4:2, Paul states it a little differently: *devote* yourselves to prayer. The word devote has as its meaning:

> To give constant attention to a thing, to give unremitting care to a thing, to persevere, to wait continually upon, to be in constant readiness for.[5]

The idea here is that the believer is to be tenacious in establishing and

---

5 Wuest, Vol. I, "Ephesians and Colossians," p. 233

maintaining a relationship based upon an open line of communication with his Lord. The believer is to demonstrate confidence that the Lord hears and answers his prayers. And if the answers do not come right away, he is to have firm resolve in order to continue his communication with his Lord.

We have as our greatest example of devotion to prayer in the person of Christ. He allotted much time in praying to His Father in heaven. Matthew Henry points out from the Gospel of Luke some of the instances of Our Lords' praying:

> When he was baptized (3:21), he was praying; he withdrew into the wilderness, and prayed (5:16); he went out into a mountain to pray, and continued all night in prayer (6:12); he was alone praying (9:18); soon after, he went up into a mountain to pray, and as he prayed he was transfigured (9:28, 29); and here (11:1) he was praying in a certain place.[6]

Also, Luke records that He prayed prior to His death in Gethsemane (22:41ff) and twice on the cross (23:34 and 23:46).

Chafer writes that His disciples duly noted His devotion to prayer:

> Discovering the Lord in prayer, the disciples are impressed with His complete devotion to the exercise of prayer, and they may have reasoned that if He who is so perfect in Himself needed to pray, how much more needful it would be for men like themselves.[7]

And it would be fitting for all believer's today to devote themselves to a life of prayer, where they are actively aware of being in His presence and consistent in conferring with Him concerning any issue of life.

---

[6] Henry, Matthew (n/d) Matthew Henry's Commentary on the Whole Bible, New York, NY: Fleming H. Revell, 5.692

[7] Chafer, *Systematic Theology*, 5.160-161

Our Approach to Prayer

The writer of the book of Hebrews instructs us concerning our approach to God in prayer.

> Therefore, let us draw near with confidence to the throne of grace, so that we may receive mercy and find grace to help in time of need. (Hebrews 4:16)

The word confidence means that we should have freedom without fear of speaking in our conversations with the Lord. There is nothing that we should keep from Him regarding our cares and concerns. Similarly, we should never feel uncomfortable in praising Him, for He is worthy to receive all of our praise and adoration. We should be comfortable in His presence and regard our relationship as genuine and intimate.

Dr. Hodge gives further details of the manner in which we are to approach God in prayer. The following is excerpts drawn from his Systematic Theology:

> *Sincerity* – God is a Spirit. He searches the heart. He is not satisfied with words, or with external homage. He cannot be deceived and will not be mocked. It is a great offence, therefore, in His sight, when we utter words before Him in which our hearts do not join.

> *Reverence* – We are required to serve Him with reverence and godly fear. And whenever heaven is opened to our view, its inhabitants are seen prostrate before the throne. We offend God, therefore, when we address Him as we would a fellow creature, or use forms of expression of undue familiarity.

> *Humility* – This includes, first, a due sense of our insignificance as creatures; and secondly, a proper apprehension of our ill-desert and uncleanness in the sight of God as sinners. It is the opposite of self-righteousness, of self-complacency and self-confidence. [Cp/w: Job 42:6 NKJV; Isa. 6:5; Luke 18:13]

Persistence – God deals with us as a wise benefactor. He requires that we should appreciate the value of the blessings for which we ask, and that we should manifest a proper earnestness of desire. [Cp/w: Luke 11:5-10; 18:1-8; Mt. 15:22-28]

Submission – Every man who duly appreciates his relation to God, will, no matter what his request, be disposed to say, "Lord, not my will but thine be done."[8]

In addition, the believer must approach God in faith. The writer to the Hebrews states this fact:

And without faith it is impossible to please Him, for he who comes to God must believe that He is and that He is the rewarder of those who seek Him. (Hebrews 11:6)[9]

It would be futile to approach God without the confidence of His existence and to ask of Him our hearts desires. However, for the believer, there is a wealth of Scriptural evidences of not only God's existence, but the witness of believers who prayed to the living God and received answers that changed their lives and glorified Him.

The Order of Prayer

Closely related to the believer's approach to prayer is the *order of how* he is to pray. Chafer rightly declares:

The right order or form of prayer is to pray to the Father in the name of the Son and through, or by the power of, the Holy Spirit.[10]

Elsewhere he adds that:

Praying to the Father in the name of the Son and in the power of the Holy Spirit is an order which has not been arbitrarily imposed. The reason for this order is quite obvious. To pray to Christ would mean to abandon His

---

[8] Hodge, 3:701-703
[9] See also 1 John 5:14
[10] Chafer, *Systematic Theology*, 5.164

mediation; it would not be praying *through* Him but rather *to* Him, thereby sacrificing the most vital feature of prayer under grace – praying *in His name*. [emphasis his][11]

The evidence to support this is to be found in Scripture:

1)   Praying to the Father

When the Lord Jesus was instructing His disciples how to pray, He established that they should begin by addressing the Father:

> *Luke 11:2* – And He said to them, "When you pray say: 'Father, hallowed be Your name.'"

Here is a clear directive from Our Lord that we are to ask *of* the Father and *in* His name:

> *John 16:23* – "In that day you will not question Me about anything. Truly, truly, I say to you, if you ask the Father for anything in My name, He will give it to you."

Our Lord, as our perfect example in life and prayer, addressed His prayers to the Father:

> *Luke 22:42* – "Father, if you are willing, remove this cup from Me."

Also, in Luke 23:46, He addressed His last prayer in this manner while He hung on the cross.

2)   In the Name of the Christ

Jesus emphasized this three times in the Gospel of John:

John 14:13-14 – Whatever you ask in My name, that will I do, so that the Father may be glorified in the Son. If you ask Me anything in My name, I will do it.

John 15:16 – You did not choose Me but I chose you, and appointed you that you would go and bear fruit, and that your fruit would remain, so that whatever you ask of the Father in My name He may give to you.

---

[11] Chafer, *Systematic Theology*, 7.253

John 16:23-24 – In that day you will not question Me about anything. Truly, truly, I say to you, if you ask the Father for anything in My name, He will give it to you. Until now you have asked for nothing in My name; ask and you will receive, so that your joy may be made full.

Dr. Chafer asserts that the believer now shares a partnership with Christ in prayer, lending itself to a common interest and mission with the Lord Jesus. He states further that:

> The very act of praying in the name of Christ is in itself an assumption that He also makes petition to the Father for those things that are in the will of God and for which the Christian prays.[12]

The operative fact is that that which is asked must be in conformance to His will.

3) *In the Power of the Spirit*

It has already been noted that Scripture directs the believer to be controlled by the Holy Spirit.[13] So it is not surprising that we are directed to pray in the power of the Spirit. What we pray for should be under the direction of the Spirit as He helps us to call to mind the proper issues of which we are to ask of the Father.

Paul states in Ephesians 6:18:

> With all prayer and petition pray at all times in the Spirit, and with this in view, be on the alert with all perseverance and petition for all the saints.

Jude echoes this:

> But you, beloved, building yourselves up on your most holy faith, praying in the Holy Spirit.[14]

Kenneth Wuest fully explains the intent of Jude 20 from the perspective of the original Greek:

---

[12] Chafer, *Systematic Theology*, 3.257
[13] Ephesians 5:18
[14] Jude 20

"In the Holy Ghost" is locative of sphere. That is, all true prayer is exercised in the sphere of the Holy Spirit, motivated and empowered by Him. That means that if the saint expects to really pray, he must be Spirit-filled or Spirit-controlled. The fullness of the Holy Spirit is the prerequisite to effectual praying. The Spirit, when yielded to, leads us in our petitions and generates within us the faith necessary to acceptable and answered prayer. The expression "praying in the Holy Ghost" is also instrumental of means. We pray by means of the Holy Spirit, in dependence upon Him.[15]

In Romans 8:26-27, the Apostle Paul speaks of an additional work of the Holy Spirit in relation to the believer's prayer:

In the same way the Spirit also helps our weakness; for we do not know how to pray as we should, but the Spirit Himself intercedes for us with groanings too deep for words; and He who searches the hearts knows what the mind of the Spirit is, because He intercedes for the saints according to the will of God.

Paul explains that there are times when the believer is under great duress concerning an issue of life or a spiritual need. It is at this time that the Holy Spirit intervenes on behalf of the believer who is unable to express his needs to the heavenly Father. The Spirit interprets the inaudible "groanings" of the believer and relays them intelligibly to the Father. These groanings are "too deep for words," or literally unutterable. They are not verbalized - they are heartfelt and inexpressible. They are the results of a weakened spiritual state. Dr. Hodge states that:

Instead of our ignorance putting a seal upon our lips, and leaving our hearts to break, the Spirit gives our desires a language heard and understood of God.[16]

Since the believer lives within a spiritual battle field, this special

---

[15] Wuest, Vol. II, "In These Last Days," p. 255
[16] Hodge, Charles (1997) *Commentary on the Epistle to the Romans*, Albany, OR: AGES Software, p. 431

intercession could be compared to what the military refers to as OPSEC (Operation Security). The idea is that the Holy Spirit utilizes a secure channel of communication to ensure that the information concerning the weakened spiritual condition of the believer is not revealed to the enemy, thus thwarting the satanic forces.[17] It is quite possible that the hymnist had this in mind when he wrote: "Satan trembles when he sees, the weakest saint upon his knees";[18] fully aware that he would be hindered in his attempt at causing the weak believer to stumble. If it were not for the power of the Holy Spirit to intercede on behalf of the believer, personal victory of the moment-by-moment walk of faith could not be fully realized.

The Conditional Elements of Prayer

There are three conditional elements which the believer should be familiar with in order to enjoy productive communication with his Lord.

First, there is a common misunderstanding concerning prayer. Many believe that the sky is the limit in what they ask. However, this is refuted in James 4:3:

> You ask and do not receive, because you ask with wrong motives, so that you may spend it on your pleasures.

There are limitations established upon believer's prayers. Prayer is not asking for simple pleasures for the believer to glory in. The main objective to answered prayer is "so that the Father may be glorified in the Son."[19] The believer's first and primary consideration of prayer is to determine if what is being asked is truly that which will ultimately glorify God. Our prayers, just as our lives, are to be solely carried

---

[17] Clough, Charles (2009) "Lesson 157 - Ascension and Session of Christ (cont.), Review Faith Rest Drill" *Part 6: New Truths of the Kingdom Aristocracy* [30May2011] http://www.bibleframework.com/bf-transcripts/Clough_Framework_157.htm

[18] Cowper, William (1826) "Exhortation to Prayer," *The Works of The Rev. John Newton,* New Haven, CT: Nathan Whiting, vol. 2, p. 549

[19] John 14:13

out in order to glorify our Lord. This is what the Apostle Paul meant in 1 Corinthians 10:31:

> Whether, then, you eat or drink or whatever you do, do all to the glory of God.

In stating this, God's provisions for our lives should not be confused at this point. There may be times of great physical needs (food, shelter, medical) of which we go to the Father in prayer. These do not fall into the category of selfish pleasures of which James speaks.

Secondly, the Lord Jesus stated in John 15:7:

> If you abide in Me, and My words abide in you, ask whatever you wish, and it will be done for you.

Here Jesus points out a condition in prayer that His words must abide in us. What does it mean to abide? The Greek word used here means "to be and remain united with,"[20] in this case, His Word. Jesus is not stating here that we should have a simplistic understanding of His Word, and then ask whatever we want, regardless as to whether what is asked conforms to His Word. We are to ask of the Father for that which coincides with His reveled Word.

Dr. Chafer comments:

> To have the words of Christ in the heart is to be informed about that which constitutes His will, or that which He elsewhere has termed "my commandments" [John 15:10]. That which constitutes His will must be comprehended before it can be undertaken.[21]

In order for our prayer requests to be scripturally accurate, we must have a thorough knowledge of His directives for our lives so that we understand His revealed plan for the ages as well as His will for our lives.

The third conditional element is that the believer's attitude in prayer should imitate that of the Lord Jesus. Luke 22:42 records that He prayed prior to His death on the cross, "Father, if You are willing,

---

[20] Zodhiates, G3306
[21] Chafer, *Systematic Theology*, 5.163

remove this cup from Me; yet not My will, but Yours be done." As much as He desired not to endure the sufferings and death of crucifixion, He did *not* resign Himself to the Father's fate[22], but He held firm to His conviction that what would take place would be based upon the Father's will, and not upon human emotion.

This is further supported by the Lord Jesus in what has become known as "The Lord's Prayer." In Matthew 6:10, Jesus taught His disciples to pray to the Father: "Your kingdom come. Your will be done, on earth as it is in heaven."

This attitude of the Lord Jesus that the Father's will is the priority of His prayers, flows over from His overall attitude of His earthly ministry. In John 6:38 Jesus stated:

> For I have come down from heaven, not to do My own will, but the will of Him who sent Me.

Believers are to have this same humble attitude demonstrated by the Lord Jesus, with regards to their overall ministry – which includes prayer – that the Father's will is to be the focal point of our lives.[23]

The Apostle John provides us with the assurance of our prayers being heard and answered when we demonstrate this same humble attitude of the Lord Jesus.

> This is the confidence which we have before Him, that, if we ask anything according to His will, He hears us. (1 John 5:14)

Summary

Prayer is the believer's intimate communication with his Lord. It

---

[22] "Prayer is killed by the heresy of fatalism. Fatalism insists that 'what will be, will be,' regardless of the means necessary to execute that which 'will be.' In the area of prayer fatalism argues that prayer effort is unnecessary because God is going to do His will anyway." Clough, Charles (2009) "Partial Restoration: The Discipline of Hope, *Part 4: Disciplinary Truths of God's Kingdom* [30 May, 2011] http://www.bibleframework.com/bf-notes/Sec_4_5.htm

[23] Philippians 2:5

should be the expression of the moment-by-moment relationship he has in Christ and guided by the Holy Spirit. At any waking moment the believer should be able and prepared to enter into conversation with God concerning any matter and have the confidence that his prayers are heard and answered. We are to pray always (1 Thessalonians 5:17), for our needs and for the needs of other believers (Ephesians 6:18; Colossians 4:3; 1 Thessalonians 5:25; 1 Timothy 2:1), for the salvation of those of our acquaintances and family members, and for our civil authorities (1 Timothy 2:2).

Prayer is not a psychological pretense that considers: "Maybe God is there, maybe He's not, but I'm not taking any chances. So I'll pray and see what happens." This would basically demonstrate a grave lack of faith. We believe that God exists, because He says so in His Word. We are to approach God boldly and at the same time with humility and reverence. Our prayers are to be directed to the Father, in the name of the Son and in the power of the Holy Spirit. And what we ask must be conditioned upon those things which bring glory to the Father, and that which conforms to His revealed will. These issues are crucial to successful prayer as supported by Scripture.

Dr. Chafer provides a fitting conclusion:

> Compliance with these conditions insures that the human will is in agreement with the divine will. Transforming things, mighty indeed, are wrought by prayer, but only such things as comport [agree, be consistent] with the will and purpose of God.[24]

THE WEALTH OF PROMISES

The last spiritual dynamic to be examined is the enormous wealth of promises that God provides for every situation in which the believer finds himself. The word promise, according to Webster, is "a declaration that gives the person to whom it is made a right to expect or to claim the performance or forbearance of a specified act."[25] The

[24] Chafer, *Systematic Theology*, 1.256
[25] *Webster's*, p. 682

certainty of a declared promise coming to fruition would depend upon the integrity of the one making the promise. Not all men are trustworthy enough to fulfill their promises. But in the case of a promise made by God, there is absolute certainty that He will not break His word. The Apostle Paul testified to this fact:

> Paul, a bond-servant of God and an apostle of Jesus Christ, for the faith of those chosen of God and the knowledge of the truth which is according to godliness, in the hope of eternal life, which God, who cannot lie, promised long ages ago. (Titus 1:1-2)

And the writer of Hebrews concurs:

> Let us hold fast the confession of our hope without wavering, for He who promised is faithful. (Hebrews 10:23)

Their Purpose

The promises of God are truths contained in His Word designed to provide stability for the believer in any given situation of life. Whether it is a disastrous and devastating event or in the midst of daily conflicts and worries, the promises of God are made available so that the believer, even while in the midst of pressure, will have confidence that his Lord is in control, and thereby will be able to endure any of the world's trials or tribulations.

The Apostle Peter wisely wrote concerning the power of God's promises for the life of the believer:

> Seeing that His divine power has granted to us everything pertaining to life and godliness, through the true knowledge of Him who called us by His own glory and excellence. For by these He has granted to us His precious and magnificent promises, so that by them you may become partakers of the divine nature, having escaped the corruption that is in the world by lust. (2 Peter 1:3-4)

His precious and magnificent promises are designed to enable the believer to become a partaker of the divine nature. Note that we do not become divine in *our* nature, but simply partakers, sharers of the power which God has incorporated in His promises. When these promises are applied correctly in our lives they provide escape from the world's corrupting influences, stability to emulate Christ in the midst of any dire situation, and the ability to enjoy the inner peace which demonstrates our total reliance and submission to the One who is ultimately in control of our lives.

This inner peace is what Jesus referred to just prior to His death:

> Peace I leave with you; My peace I give to you; not as the world gives do I give to you. Do not let your heart be troubled, nor let it be fearful. (John 14:27)

This peace is based upon a genuine belief that since God was able to provide us with salvation through His Son, that He is able to provide "everything pertaining to life and godliness." And this means that regardless of how grim the situation might be He has decisive control of any problematic situation.

His Peace

The basic meaning of the word "peace" as metaphorically used in the New Testament is a "peace of mind, tranquility, arising from reconciliation with God and a sense of a divine favor."[26] Before trusting Christ as savior, the believer was once considered an enemy of God[27], but now since being reconciled with Him, salvation affects the whole man, to the core of his psyche. Prior to salvation he had no relationship with his Creator, so not only was he faced with eternal damnation but there was incompleteness in his being. But now, as Paul writes, "having been justified by faith, we have peace with God through our Lord Jesus Christ."[28]

Since the conflict between the believer and God is now ended, His promises are designed to engage the believer to rest confidently in a loving, trusting relationship with His Lord. This inner peace is not

---

[26] Zodhiates, G1515
[27] Romans 5:10
[28] Romans 5:1

a feeling, even though one may react with joy and praise. Lenski comments on this:

> The security and the well-being intended by this peace relate to far more than to protection in the hour of danger; they refer to the relation of the disciples to God. "Peace" is a central concept and should not be reduced by being in some way turned into mere feeling.[29]

The successful implementation of God's promises will provide stability and peace for the believer. As already described, it is an inner peace of mind in which the believer demonstrates his reliance upon God's competent control of every event of life. Paul writes of this peace:

> And the peace of God, which surpasses all comprehension, will guard your hearts and your minds in Christ Jesus. (Philippians 4:7)

Scripture likens this peace to the rest of God, where God ceased from His work of creation.[30] Ryrie points this out from his notes on Hebrews 4:9:

> The word in verse 9 (*rest*) indicates that, just as God ceased from His creative activity on the seventh day (v. 4), so believers may cease from working for their salvation and self-reliance in sanctification.[31]

The believer is to do likewise and cease from working – utilizing his human viewpoint to resolve the conflicts of life and to attain this rest of peace. It is not a resignation to fatalism – a "whatever will be - will be" mentality. Nor is it a psychological mind game. Fatalism and psychological mind games depict the casual relationship many believers have with God. This is not a casual relationship in which we talk to God at only certain times; go to church to say "hello" on holidays; or in the midst of trials, pull out our God to do a trick in order to get us out of a jam. This is a real moment-by-moment, 24/7

---

[29] Lenski, 4.1017

[30] Genesis 2:2

[31] Ryrie, *Ryrie Study Bible*, p. 1949, *note* 4:5-9

relationship with *the* God of the universe. Just as He ably provided eternal life through His Son, He now provides "everything[32] pertaining to life and godliness" for the believer by His promise of a rest of peace.

Promise Technique

The writer of the book of Hebrews in chapters 3 and 4 likens the provision of a rest of peace made to believers today with the promise made to the children of Israel of a promised rest in a land flowing with milk and honey.[33] However, the writer is concerned that believers might fail to secure for themselves this promised rest just as the generation of Israelites who wandered for forty years in the wilderness. These, the writer states, hardened their hearts (3:8), tested the Lord (3:9), and provoked Him (3:15). The Lord swore that "they shall not enter My rest (3:11)." And as the writer explains further "that they were not able to enter because of unbelief (3:19)."

Beginning in chapter 4, he warns believers today:

> Therefore, let us fear if, while a promise remains of entering His rest, any one of you may seem to have come short of it. For indeed we have had good news preached to us, just as they also; but the word they heard did not profit them, because it was not united by faith in those who heard. (Hebrews 4:1-2)

The writer to the Hebrews provides us with the technique for securing the promises of God by explaining that the key is to *unite* God's promises with faith. The King James Version uses the word "mix" instead of unite, which lends itself nicely to the idea of a recipe. This is the recipe for successful utilization of the promises of God: the promises mixed with faith produces the means by which the believer is able to attain inner peace for his moment-by-moment walk of faith. So that when he is confronted with conflicts and turmoil he doesn't fall apart or become twisted up inside but is able

---

[32] "Everything" means everything!
[33] Exodus 3:8

to think clearly and rest in the secure relationship that he has with his Lord. He knows that this battle belongs to the Lord,[34] and that He is able to handle every situation, even death. When the believer is totally confident of his eternal destiny, he is able to conquer his fear of death. And if death is the worst case scenario, than nothing else can destabilize the life of the believer.

Application

This technique of mixing the promises with faith can be utilized in any situation. Whether it is danger of death, personal conflicts, or the death of a loved one, claiming God's promises for the appropriate situation is the means by which the believer demonstrates his faith in God's ability to meet the challenges of the Christian life. It is not that the believer sits back and does nothing in the midst of trials. He still must respond to the immediate situation at hand. However, claiming the appropriate promise allows him to have a clear mind to think Biblically straight without the debilitating emotions, confident that the Lord will see him through. The end situation may not be altogether to his liking, but he will have the assurance that God will honor His word and provide the peace of mind and strength to carry on.

The following are a select few of the many promises which God has provided for believers.

Peace

> Isaiah 26:3 - The steadfast of mind You will keep in perfect peace, because he trusts in You.

Strength in Waiting

> Isaiah 40:31 - Yet those who wait for the Lord will gain new strength; They will mount up with wings like eagles, They will run and not get tired, They will walk and not become weary.

Assurance that God is in Control

---

[34] 1 Samuel 17:47; 2 Chronicles 20:15

Romans 8:28 - And we know that God causes all things to work together for good to those who love God, to those who are called according to His purpose.

In the Midst of Crisis-Conflict

Psalm 55:22 – Cast [hurl] your burden upon the Lord and He will sustain you; He will never allow the righteous to be shaken.

1 Peter 5:7 – Casting all your anxiety on Him, because He cares for you.

The student of God's Word would do well to catalog, memorize, and avail himself to these promises specifically designed to benefit him in his daily walk of faith.

THE GRACE OF GOD

At this point it would be beneficial to consider the Biblical principle of grace, since the dynamics examined in this chapter and chapter 11, exemplify the truth of God's grace provision for the believer in time.

The Greek word for grace is *charis* (χάρις), meaning graciousness or favor. Zodhiates notes that it implies "A favor done without expectation of return."[35] He goes on to assert that in reference to God it is:

The absolutely free expression of the loving kindness of God to men finding its only motive in the bounty and benevolence of the Giver.[36]

Although grace is not an attribute of God, it is His love and mercy at work. The saving of a soul, as noted in chapter 9, is by the grace of God, not by any work of man (Eph. 2:8-9). It is because of the love of God (John 3:16) and according to His mercy (Titus 3:5) that

---

[35] Zodhiates, S. (2000, c1992, c1993). *The Complete Word Study Dictionary: New Testament* (electronic ed.) (G5485). Chattanooga, TN: AMG Publishers.

[36] Ibid., Zodhiates

He reached out to provide salvation for man, by the work of Christ on the cross.

After salvation, in spite of the believer's faults, God's grace provision continues. His forgiveness of the personal sins of the believer after salvation is His grace provision of cleansing and making the believer fit to serve. The indwelling Holy Spirit is His grace provision of empowerment in and through the believer in order to produce divine good. His grace provision of answering prayers becomes the basis for a real relationship with the believer. And His grace provision of the promises of His Word equips believers to trust and to rely upon Him in every situation.

Grace is God working to accomplish His purpose in our lives. The believer must understand God's purpose for his life and yield himself to operate within the boundaries of God's grace provisions. When the believer decides to do God's work outside of the empowerment of the Holy Spirit, it is no longer grace at work. When the believer fails to confess sin and relies on some form of penance, it is no longer grace. When we utilize our own means to handle difficult situations in life, instead of claiming His promises or consulting Him in prayer, we are no longer operating under the grace principle of God. We are relying on our own power, and consequently, we do not advance in the Christian life.

How is the believer to advance in the Christian life? Paul explains:

> For the grace of God has appeared, bringing salvation to all men, instructing us to deny ungodliness and worldly desires and to live sensibly, righteously and godly in the present age. (Titus 2:11-12)

Chafer comments on this verse:

> The passage reveals...that it is the same grace which has brought salvation to all men, that teaches *us*...The teachings of grace, it will be found, comprise all of the teachings of the Epistles, the Acts, and also certain

portions of the Gospels apart from their mere historical features [emphasis his].[37]

Just as the believer responded to the grace provision of salvation, he must respond to the grace provision of instruction in doctrine in order to advance and reach his spiritual growth potential. He must not allow his failures to stop his advance, but instead rely upon *all* of the grace provisions that will guide him through life, moment-by-moment. This requires a diligence and desire to study God's Word. The satanically influenced world about us, is outflanking Christians everywhere. They aggressively teach their belief systems in our schools, colleges, media, and entertainment industry. In Christianity today, there is very little enthusiasm for persistent and attentiveness to grace teachings, and unfortunately it is demonstrated by the fading memory of Christian principles in our culture.

CONCLUSION

The purity of life for the believer is of great importance in order to counteract the unbelief and anti-Christian characteristics in this present day culture. Believers today must shed the notion that the relationship with their Lord is of a casual nature. He is to be the central personage of their lives. As with any healthy relationship, the believer should have a desire to please his Lord and to glorify Him with his life. The dynamics examined in this chapter and chapter 11, provide a power base for the believer in order to fully accommodate him in his spiritual endeavor. The forgiveness and cleansing of personal sins remedies the interrupted fellowship with the Lord and enables the believer for service. This is the key to true spirituality – a believer controlled by the Holy Spirit and producing works which honor and glorify God. Consistent prayer keeps the channels of communication open as the believer demonstrates his reliance on his Lord for everything. And the wealth of God's promises provides the believer with the proper response of inner peace to any crisis situation and the security of a caring and loving heavenly Father.

---

[37] Chafer, *Systematic Theology*, 4.182-183

With the mastery of these spiritual skills, the believer can become a powerful witness to the world.

CHAPTER CHECK

1. What attitudes of the believer's heart will achieve open and intelligent prayer?

2. When and where should the believer pray?

3. Explain the Biblical order of prayer and why it is designed this way.

4. Are there any conditions for prayer? Explain them.

5. For what reason(s) has God provided promises to the believer?

6. Describe the technique for appropriating God's promises.

7. Give some examples of how God's promises have helped you.

⚘ 13 ⚘

THE PRACTICE OF A PURIFIED LIFE

The dynamics of the Christian life as outlined in the last two chapters provides the empowerment necessary for the believer to live a life which honors and glorifies his Lord. The successful influence of Christianity upon today's culture is dependent upon each believer utilizing these dynamics moment-by-moment, in synchronization with all believers who comprise the universal church, the Body of Christ.

So far this study has established these main beliefs: 1) that there is an unseen conflict within the world system controlled by Satan which opposes God; 2) that the universal church, the Body of Christ, is comprised of all those who have trusted in Christ as Savior, regardless of local church affiliations; 3) that the church, even though it is not of this world, must maintain a witness for Christ in the world; 4) that there is a need for the church to return to the foundations of Christianity – the authority of Scripture, and unified and indisputable doctrine; 5) that the believer should live a purified life and is provided with the dynamics to accomplish this objective. The aim of this chapter is to demonstrate how the Biblical principles previously explained in this study should be implemented so that believers will reach their spiritual growth potential, enabling them to become effective witnesses within this present evil culture.

CHRISTIAN LOVE

The directive to love the brethren is a theme implicated by the various writers of the New Testament. It would be good to quote a few of them.

1 John 4:7 - Beloved, let us love one another, for love is from God; and everyone who loves is born of God and knows God.

1 Peter 1:22 - Since you have in obedience to the truth purified your souls for a sincere love of the brethren, fervently love one another from the heart.

James 2:8 - If, however, you are fulfilling the royal law according to the Scripture, "you shall love your neighbor as yourself," you are doing well.

Romans 12:10a - Be devoted to one another in brotherly love.

Hebrews 13:1 - Let love of the brethren continue.

It is unfortunate that our culture is still suffering from the ill effects of the 60's and 70's Jesus freak movement that took as one of their mantras: "God is love."[1] It is indeed true that God is love, but not the type of love that was espoused by the hippies. They were merely interested in the simple manifestations of the human emotions of sex and mutual admiration. The love of God is an attribute of His character. This is the love which believers are asked to emulate – a love that is not seeking something in return; an attitude instead of an emotion. This does not mean that our giving of love is cold and emotionless. The emotions may be a legitimate response, but it is not the feeling which the believer aspires to achieve, it is the desire to express the selfless characteristic of the love of God towards other believers.

This demonstration of love to other believers may be varied depending on the spiritual gifts given to believers. For instance: helps, the provision of personal needs (food, shelter, and clothing); giving of money; teaching, so other may grow,[2] to name a few.

---

[1] An atrocious misinterpretation and misapplication of 1 John 4:16
[2] See Romans 12:4-8

Christian love should be towards all believers, regardless of local church affiliations, or perceived doctrinal differences. And this should be so, not because it would be pleasant or that it would make us feel good all over. We love the brethren because we are commanded to do so by our Lord, and for a specific purpose which serves His ends. Jesus tells us:

> A new commandment I give to you, that you love one another; as I have loved you, that you also love one another. By this all will know that you are My disciples, if you have love for one another. (John 13:34-35)

He tells us that when we love one another, *all* will know that we are His disciples. This is the witness to the world which we are to provide, that we indeed are His disciples because we demonstrate love for the brethren. Our love is to be without hypocrisy, without a surface affection and an inner hatred or despising. It should be devoid of self gain or puffed up pride or a "better than thou" attitude. It should be ready to serve and to serve alongside each other on the battleground of the world. There is a battle going on around us, and we don't need a conflict within our own camp that divides and dishonors our Lord.

CHRISTIAN UNITY

Closely related to the principle of Christian love is the demonstration of unity within the Body of Christ. Where Christian love may not always be a reality, the unity of the Body of Christ is already a reality. However, it is not the responsibility of the universal church to unite the body – that has already been established by the Father. The responsibility of the universal church is to *demonstrate* unity by their doctrine and the leading of the Holy Spirit, and not by mere verbal assent.

Paul defines this unity in Ephesians 4:4-6 as one body, with one Spirit (an identical empowerment of the Holy Spirit through His gifts and leading), one hope (one confidant expectation of God's faithful fulfillment of His promises for today and for eternity), one faith (one system of doctrinal truth), one baptism (the same identifying characteristic of our union with Christ), and one God and Father of all. And again, the reason we are to demonstrate this unity within Christianity is for a singular purpose which serves the Lord Jesus. Jesus prayed to the Father:

> I do not ask on behalf of these alone, but for those also who believe in Me through their word; that they may all be one; even as You, Father, are in Me and I in You, that they also may be in Us, so that the world may believe that You sent Me. (John 17: 20-21)

Regarding this powerful statement of Jesus', Francis Schaeffer has described this as the final apologetic for the universal church.[3] Jesus asserts that the world has the right to determine that He was sent by the Father on the basis of whether Christians demonstrate unity. In other words, the unbelieving element of the world could just simply look around at Christians and if they see disunity, dissention and division, then they had the right to conclude that the God of the Bible *did not* send His Son, to die on the cross, be raised from the dead, and provide salvation for all mankind. There was a time when the world actually looked to the Christian church for the answers of morality and godliness, and for the salvation of their soul. But sadly those days are gone. The world of unbelievers and agnostics have already looked and saw the disunity, dissention and divisions which produced only a confusing witness of the God of the Bible, and now they are turned off by Christianity. There are too many divisions. There is no unified doctrine. There is dissention within the ranks. A battalion going to battle with dissention within the ranks will surely lose. The lost of the world looks at Christianity in this manner, and is rightfully disgusted.

Citing that this widespread disruption of Christian unity is inspired by Satan, Dr. Chafer writes:

> Every device of Satan is abroad to distort an outward manifestation to the world of this unity. All sectarian divisions of the church, like the theory of a partial rapture,

---

[3] Schaeffer, 4.188-190

are violence against this unity and are branded by the Apostle as the fundamental sin which causes carnality (cf. 1 Cor. 3:1-4; John 17:21-23; Eph. 4:1-4).[4]

How do we become unified? The answer is easier said than done. But it begins by returning to the foundations of the Christian faith. It will take believers across denominational lines to humbly submit to the clear teachings of Scripture and, as Paul instructs us, to endeavor to keep the unity of the Spirit:

> Therefore I, the prisoner of the Lord, implore you to walk in a manner worthy of the calling with which you have been called, with all humility and gentleness, with patience, showing tolerance for one another in love, being diligent to preserve the unity of the Spirit in the bond of peace. There is one body and one Spirit, just as also you were called in one hope of your calling; one Lord, one faith, one baptism, one God and Father of all who is over all and through all and in all. (Ephesians 4:1-6)

If the church were to truly display a unified front to this lost generation, we would not have to answer the question of whether the coming of Christ to the earth in the form of man and dying on the cross for the sins of all humanity really happened in history. The unity in all aspects of our faith would be the definitive answer.

THE FAMILY

In the 20th Century, the divine institution of the family in the United States was undermined by the unbelieving culture. The Cold War era generated the desire for personal peace and prosperity at any cost. The desire to earn higher wages in order to live like the rich and famous drove the middle-class to work longer hours and the traditional family deteriorated. Families used to wake together, eat together (at least breakfast and dinner) and to sleep usually at the same hours of the night. But with the craving to have more, businesses extended hours of operation, added shifts and eventually,

---

[4] Chafer, 4.418

many began to operate 24 hours a day, 7 days a week. The man of the house had predominately been the sole bread-winner, but in order to "survive" there was a demand for two incomes. The family became fragmented, with less time spent together and very little in common.

The first thing to go was often the moral direction for their lives. Without the father to point them in the right direction and to lead by godly example, the family members were left to devise their own system of morality based upon the standards of the unbelieving culture. Soon, Christians began to get caught up in the allure of materialism. It didn't help that the watered down doctrinal teaching of liberal theology of the late 19th and early 20th Centuries failed to rebuke this cultural trend.

The question then is: What are the Biblical directives for the Christian family? Many Biblically informed and well intentioned books have been written on this subject. This doesn't mean that they should be ignored. However, for this study, the primary source of information will be drawn from the Scriptures.

First of all, the Scriptures never speak of the family as anything other than a husband and a wife and their children.[5] The notion of same-sex marriages or unions is totally without Scriptural support. It should be reiterated here that cultural perspectives *do not* dictate Biblical doctrine. Biblical beliefs are grounded in the authoritative revelation of Scripture.[6]

Husbands

Concerning the husbands, Paul writes a command in Ephesians 5:25: "Husbands, love your wives, just as Christ also loved the church and gave Himself up for her." At first glance this doesn't seem to be too farfetched. However, when we look closely at the love which Christ has for His church, we see that it is devoid of the romanticism and sexuality between a husband and a wife. So this

---

[5] Ephesians 5:22-6:4; 1 Peter 3:1-7
[6] 2 Timothy 3:16-17

obviously means that Christ's love is on a different scale, and if we look further in Scripture, we will find that this love is truly the most difficult to imitate. The utmost level of Christ's love is to give His life for the church. The husband must be willing to do likewise for his wife. However, while the chance of this occurring is rather slim, still the other levels of Christ's example of love are likewise challenging. He forgives (Colossians 1:14), He freely gives (Romans 8:32), He provides strength and stability (Philippians 4:13), and He also keeps us securely (1 John 5:18). It is this last feature of His love that is very crucial to the marriage relationship: security.

Peter writes that the husband is to show honor to his wife "as a fellow heir of the grace of life" (1 Peter 3:7). This is a clear description of an equal and harmonious relationship, with the husband as the spiritual leader of the relationship. This does not mean that the wife has no say in the direction of the family. The smart husband will always seek the counsel of his wife, but the final decision is his, for he is to be held responsible before the Lord.

The husband, as the children's father, is further commanded to "bring them up in the discipline and instruction of the Lord".[7] The meaning from the Greek of the phrase "bring them up" implies "to nourish...to bring up to maturity."[8] He is to nourish them in the discipline and instruction of the Lord. Of this word "discipline", Dr. Vincent states that:

> The term here covers all the agencies which contribute to moral and spiritual training.[9]

The agencies implied may include chastisement (i.e. spankings) when necessary in order to produce correction.

By instruction it is meant, according to Bishop Trench:

> It is the training by word – by the word of encouragement, when this is sufficient, but also by that of remonstrance

---

[7] Ephesians 6:4
[8] Zodhiates, G1625
[9] Vincent, 3.404

[a forceful argument], of reproof, of blame, where these may be required.[10]

Although the training of the children is shared by the husband and wife, the husband is given the responsibility to ensure the proper rearing of the children.

Wives

Since God is not a God of confusion,[11] order has been initiated in the family. The wives, as both Paul and Peter state, are to "be subject to your own husbands".[12] Paul goes on to explain that this order in the family is just like in the church:

> For the husband is the head of the wife, as Christ also is the head of the church, He Himself being the Savior of the body.[13]

This might seem out of line with the conventional wisdom of the culture today, but that is because this verse has been consistently misused and misapplied. First of all, this verse is intended *for* wives, not for a husband to use as a club demanding to be the boss. Secondly, the apostles are *not* inferring that wives are inferior to husbands because they are to submit to their husbands. For the husband to be the boss, dictator, or tyrant over the wife is the furthest thing from the clear teachings of Scripture. The husband is to esteem his wife as an equal partner and to love and respect her and supply all of her needs in their relationship.[14]

What is to be understood by this verse is that there is a divinely instituted order for the family, which will allow for an organized approach to the spiritual nourishing of every family member. This is compared to the order within the Body of Christ: Christ is the

---

[10] Trench, p. 112
[11] 1 Corinthians 14:33, 40
[12] Ephesians 5:22; cp./w 1 Peter 3:1
[13] Ephesians 5:23
[14] Ephesians 5:25-29

head of the church and from Him all members receive their spiritual sustenance form Him.

Children

Paul turns his attention to the children with this command:

> Children, obey your parents in the Lord, for this is right. Honor your father and mother (which is the first commandment with a promise), so that it may be well with you, and that you may live long on the earth. (Ephesians 6:1-3)

The directive that children are to obey their parents is not an isolated truth; it is repeated in Colossians 3:20:

> Children, be obedient to your parents in all things, for this is well-pleasing to the Lord.

This command that children obey and honor their parents is an echoing of the commandment given to Moses in Exodus 20:12 and repeated in Deuteronomy 5:16. As Paul mentions, this command comes with the promise that "it may be well with you, and that you may live long on the earth." It is not too difficult to understand how a child with good training and one who readily complies with parental instruction could do well in life and live longer. Both of these elements must come together, and when they do, "this is well-pleasing to the Lord." And on the basis of pleasing God, children are blessed with a long and wonderful life.

Summary

Every Christian family knows how difficult it is working against the evil influences of this world. There are legal proceedings taking place within our culture attempting to re-define marriage as simply a union of two consenting individuals committed to a relationship, regardless of their sex. Governmental agencies are overextending their boundaries by intruding upon parental rights over their children. These attacks upon the divine institution has devastated our culture to the point that even the roles for husbands and wives have been distorted, and children are set at odds against parental authority. Not to mention that divorce is so common, that there seems to be very little reason for some to even obtain a legal marriage. Someone once theorized how impossible it would be to achieve world peace between two countries when one considers that in the majority of marriages two people couldn't even get along.

Paul enumerates in 2 Timothy 3:1-5 some of the warnings signs of the end of this age:

> But realize this, that in the last days difficult times will come. For men will be **lovers of self, lovers of money**, boastful, arrogant, **revilers, disobedient to parents, ungrateful, unholy, unloving, irreconcilable**, malicious gossips, **without self-control**, brutal, **haters of good**, treacherous, **reckless, conceited, lovers of pleasure rather than lovers of God, holding to a form of godliness, although they have denied its power**; Avoid such men as these. [emphasis added]

The bold type characteristics in the preceding verses are indicative of some of the problems within the family unit today. Even believers have been caught up in this cultural wave of rebelliousness towards God with regards to His divine plan for marriage and the family. Paul states that these are the warning signs of the end of this age. It would be well for all believers to heed his warning, avoiding such people like this and striving not to become like them in our manner of life. The church is to be the leader and example to the world with our righteous living. It begins with the individual in a right relationship with God and is carried on into the family.

WITNESSING

Just as Israel was chosen to be a witness for God to the heathen nations and just as the Apostles had been commissioned to bear witness of Christ and make disciples of men, the church of Jesus

Christ is to be a witness for Christ before a fallen world.[15] This is to be accomplished both collectively and individually. The degree of success in the witnessing of the universal church is directly dependent upon *every* believer being actively involved. This is one of the reasons why the church in the last century lost the attention of the world – the lack of a unified witness for Jesus Christ.

Paul wrote in Ephesians 2:10:

> For we are His workmanship, created in Christ Jesus for good works, which God prepared beforehand so that we would walk in them.

It is the responsibility of *all* believers to perform the work of witnessing. Paul further states in Ephesians 4:11-12 that believers are to be trained for this service. Chafer writes:

> The revelation here is not only of the fact that the saints have a witnessing service to perform, but also the fact that they are to be equipped for this service by the gifted men whom God has placed over them as their leaders.[16]

Our witness should be more than passing out Gospel tracts and literature or learning and refining an approach to presenting the Gospel. These endeavors are not to be condemned, but there is a far greater methodology for the church to employ: the infiltration of our culture with believers who not only live an exemplary life of faith, but who infuse their beliefs into every area of our culture – business, politics, education, charity, arts and entertainment.

Biblical truths ought to be the guiding force of our culture. Therefore, it becomes the responsibility of believers to adhere to God's standards and to allow His standards to direct their actions and their input into every discipline of life, without compromise. To compromise God's standards is error. To attempt to synchronize godless cultural standards with Biblical truth is compromise at the worst level and sinful.

---

[15] 2 Corinthians 5:18-20
[16] Chafer, Systematic Theology, 4.68-69

The Christian businessman (small or corporate) is to be ethical in conducting his responsibilities; honest with all associates; compassionate with all. The Christian politician governs and enacts laws with godly integrity. The Christian instructor teaches objective truths based upon that which finds cohesiveness in the Word of God. In other words, the Christian in every discipline of culture is an ever present witness for Christ, not just in word, but his influence permeates Biblical truth within each profession. The world should recognize that he is a Christian and that his life is based upon the standards of God's Word, and that he is not going to compromise Biblical standards.

This is the totality of Christian witnessing: soul winning for Christ as well as an influential representation of Christianity in every discipline of life.

Civic and Social Responsibilities

Christians should be the most active and knowledgeable citizens – as to how our government works, both local and national, and possess a firm understanding of our history and how we have gained and maintained the freedoms which we now possess. This should enable the believer to be Biblically informed for voting governing officials and voicing opinions. Believers who shun the ballot box or refuse to understand the issues of society, whether consciously or unconsciously, thrust aside a potential opportunity to impact their society for good. Instead, they allow a godless culture to rob them of their rights and freedoms. Freedom in a society is an important factor which allows the unhindered presentation of the Gospel, the freedom of the individual to hear and accept Christ as Savior, and limitless ability to worship God.

There is an old adage which suggests that in polite company, one should *not* discuss religion or politics. This is a clever assault upon Christianity and freedom – an attempt to minimize the witness of Christ and to rob the citizens of their personal rights. What Christians should be doing is discussing openly the truth of Jesus Christ and discussing civic issues which maintain personal rights and freedom for all. Believers should be active in calling and writing their representatives, or writing newspaper editorials, to express their viewpoints.

If our elected officials are unbelievers, than believers are to pray for their salvation. Paul speaks of this:

> First of all, then, I urge that entreaties and prayers, petitions and thanksgivings, be made on behalf of all men, for kings and all who are in authority, so that we may lead a tranquil and quiet life in all godliness and dignity. (1 Timothy 2:1-2)

Pentecost explains why:

> In the New Testament the church is instructed to pray for governmental authorities, since they are God-appointed, so that those in authority may be saved and the saints live in peace as a result.[17]

Instead of complaining about the apparent evils of the judicial system, the misguided politician, or the anti-God education system, we should pray for these people that they will be saved and that we may all live peaceably.

EDUCATION

Another area of society in which believers ought to be actively involved is the public school system. The liberal's erroneous notion of the separation of church and state has left the education of our children in the hands of those wanting to eradicate the Christian heritage of our nation. The public school could be likened to the prison system in the United States today. Prison inmates often learn nothing more than how to hone their criminal trade. Public school children often learn nothing more than the subjective, liberal agenda – socialism, evolution, entitlement. School rules and policies have deteriorated over the past 50 years. The lack of discipline from dress standards to classroom decorum is a clear demonstration that

---

[17] Pentecost, p.210

the "inmates" are in control. It doesn't help matters when parents support the attempts of teachers and administrators to make school "contemporary" or more palatable for the students. These efforts have led to a dearth of serious and objective education – especially in the areas of history, science, government and sociology, along with a grossly exaggerated emphasis upon athletic programs.

What is the Christian parent who truly desires a godly education for his child to do? First, there must be solid Biblical training in the home. This is the first line of defense for the child who is to be confronted with the realities of a godless education system as well as the culture in general. Secondly, the Christian has two options at this point: 1) to take back the public school system.[18] The Christian should be in the leadership roles of the PTA or PTO, the teacher's union, the school board, they should be principals and teachers. Christians should hold their governments accountable for using the public purse for teaching the godlessness of this culture. If this had been the case 50 years ago, our schools would not have eliminated Christian principles and values; or 2) to join forces with all Christians to remove our children from the public school system altogether. If we believe that it is essential for our children to receive a godly education, than we should demonstrate our conviction and build our own schools.

The fact is that we as believers have a responsibility before the fallen culture, to be active in the leadership roles of our government, in business and in the education of our children – being Biblically sound with our ballot box decisions and maintaining a powerful voice in the public arena. If the world considers us to be radicals, then so be it; just as long as we tenaciously uphold the Word of God.

---

[18] Note: "The first schools in America were clearly the fruits of the Protestant Revolt in Europe. The reformers everywhere had insisted upon the necessity of the Gospels as a means to personal salvation. This meant, carried to its logical conclusion, that each child, girls as well as boys, should be taught to read so that they might become acquainted with the commandments of God and learn what was demanded of them." Cubberly, Ellwood P. (1919) *Public Education in the United States*, Houghton Mifflin: Boston, MA, p.13

Conclusion

To become effective witnesses and to assume leadership roles within the culture, each believer must begin to follow our Lord's directive of love towards fellow believers and a clear-cut demonstration of unity (one Lord, one faith, etc.) with *all* who claim Christ as Savior. This as a necessity must cut across denominational lines.

Additionally, the Christian family must demonstrate a renewed solidarity based upon the Biblical principles related to this divine institution: Maintaining the basis of the marriage union of man and woman; the rightful administration of responsibilities; the nurturing of children with Biblical principles; the right response of children to parents.

And finally, the believer, even though he is considered an enemy in the world, he must still take an active role in the culture: at the ballot box; a voice in the public arena; in the work place; and in the education of our children.

The Apostle Paul furnishes definitive instructions pertaining to our lives, when implemented they will be a solid Biblical influence in our culture:

> Let love be without hypocrisy. Abhor what is evil; cling to what is good. Be devoted to one another in brotherly love; give preference to one another in honor; not lagging behind in diligence, fervent in spirit, serving the Lord; rejoicing in hope, persevering in tribulation, devoted to prayer, contributing to the needs of the saints, practicing hospitality. Bless those who persecute you; bless and do not curse. Rejoice with those who rejoice, and weep with those who weep. Be of the same mind toward one another; do not be haughty in mind, but associate with the lowly. Do not be wise in your own estimation. Never pay back evil for evil to anyone. Respect what is right in the sight of all men. If possible, so far as it depends on you, be at peace with all men. Never take your own revenge, beloved, but leave room for the wrath of God, for it is written,

"Vengeance is Mine, I will repay," says the Lord. "But if your enemy is hungry, feed him, and if he is thirsty, give him a drink; for in so doing you will heap burning coals on his head." Do not be overcome by evil, but overcome evil with good. (Romans 12:9-21)

Let us each examine our relations within the culture and compare ourselves with Paul's directive to see if we are in agreement with Biblical standards and if not, we must adjust and restructure our ways and our thinking.

CHAPTER CHECK

1. Describe the type of love that the Bible instructs believers to engender.

2. Explain the unity which Christians are to demonstrate.

3. How would this benefit the cause of Christianity?

4. What are the Biblical commands for husbands, wives and children?

5. How are Biblical family values evidenced in our culture today?

6. What are the methods of witnessing to those who are without Christ?

7. How should the Christian fulfill his civic responsibility?

8. In what ways does the public school system deter godly education?

9. What should be the Christian's response?

ᨠ Epilogue ᨟

THE LAST WORD AND APPEAL

This study began by establishing the basis for the unseen battle between the God of the Bible and the world system influenced by Satan. It was further determined that the church of Jesus Christ is presently at center stage of this conflict. This battle has been a fundamental truth of Christianity for centuries. Concerning this battle, Francis Schaeffer states:

> As Christians, we say we live in a *supernatural universe* and that there is a battle, since the fall of man, and that this battle is in both the seen and the unseen world. This is what we say we believe [emphasis his].[1]

Schaeffer seems to imply that although we as Christians may "*say* we believe" in this battle, we really haven't demonstrated that we *believe* it. Each believer should be aware of this battle between the ruler of this world, Satan, and Jesus Christ. Since believers are in union with Christ, we too are entangled in this on-going battle. Again, Schaeffer points this out:

> Make no mistake. We as Bible-believing evangelical Christians are locked in a battle. This is not a friendly gentleman's discussion. It is a life and death conflict between the spiritual hosts of wickedness and those who claim the name of Christ. It is a conflict on the level of ideas between

---

[1] Schaeffer, 3.208

two fundamentally opposed views of truth and reality. It is a conflict on the level of actions between a complete moral perversion and chaos and God's absolutes.[2]

Granted that some are indeed aware of this fact, the sad commentary is that the vast majority of believers are totally oblivious. If they truly were aware, then there would be a concerted effort to combat the evil influence upon Christianity and our culture. But instead, Christianity today is caught up in sectarian and doctrinal divisions. This study addressed this issue and provided a solution based solely upon Divine viewpoint: the authority of Scripture.

The local church should be primarily a schoolhouse; teaching men, women and children the precepts of God's Word and exhorting them to imitate Christ and to produce the will of God by the empowerment of the Holy Spirit. Dr. Chafer elaborates upon this:

> This end result, which is doing the whole will of God, is not accomplished in all Christians or by virtue of the fact that they are saved, but only in those among the saved ones who "walk not after the flesh, but after the Spirit." The contrast is between those Christians who depend on their own human resources...and those Christians who depend upon the power of the indwelling Spirit.[3]

Unfortunately, in many well intentioned churches, someone may become a Christian on Sunday night and then be instructed to join in the Monday night witnessing program. It is a good thing to want believers to become involved in Spiritual service, but they must have adequate training and be advancing to reach their spiritual growth potential prior to service. Hymn sessions, choir ensembles, contemporary bands, dramas, testimonies, board meetings, etc., should be secondary to the teaching of doctrine in the local church. This necessitates that the pastor-teacher must spend the majority of his time studying God's Word. He is then to train his flock to do the work of service (i.e. visit the sick, feed and shelter the needy, and be

---

[2] Schaeffer, 4.316
[3] Chafer, *Systematic Theology*, 6.199-200

effective witnesses in every area of society). The individual believer is to devote his time to study, prayer and living a moment-by-moment life where the person of Christ is infused into every area of his life.

Doctrine first and foremost is the need of every believer if we are to succeed in doing the whole will of God. Dr. Wuest comments on the correct process:

> Doctrine must always precede exhortation since in doctrine the saint is shown his exalted position which makes the exhortation to a holy life, a reasonable one, and in doctrine, the saint is informed as to the resources of grace he possesses with which to obey the exhortations.[4]

The exhortation which Dr. Wuest is referring to is for believers to obey the divine directive to do the "work of service," by utilizing the doctrine that the pastor-teacher has equipped him with.[5] It cannot be stressed more vigorously: the pulpit ministry of the church today must become more centered on teaching the foundational principles of our Christian faith, coupled with the practical application of how we are to exhibit the character of Christ before a lost and dying culture. Sermons of exhortations without doctrine and feel-good sermons should be done away with, and replaced with that which will equip and build up the body of Christ. The Apostle Paul provides the results of this type of teaching:

> Until we all attain to the unity of the faith and of the knowledge of the Son of God, to mature manhood, to the measure of the stature of the fullness of Christ, so that we may no longer be children, tossed to and fro by the waves and carried about by every wind of doctrine, by human cunning, by craftiness in deceitful schemes. Rather, speaking the truth in love, we are to grow up in every way into him who is the head, into Christ, from whom the whole body, joined and held together by every joint with which it is equipped, when each part is working

---

4 Wuest, Vol. I, "Romans," p. 204
5 Ephesians 4:12

properly, makes the body grow so that it builds itself up in love. (Ephesians 4:13-16 ESV)

The appeal is for Christian leaders – in seminaries, denominations, local churches – and to all believers everywhere: First, to strive to demonstrate the unity of the Body of Christ with unity of doctrine, without compromise or accommodation to cultural inducement. Secondly, to practice a visible love among all Christians who claim Christ as their Savior and who hold tenaciously to the authority of Scripture. And thirdly, to become actively involved in the unseen battle that is all about us. To ignore its reality or to shy away from the conflict spells certain defeat and dishonor to our Lord. To engage in this battle, in the power of the Holy Spirit, means victory and glory for Jesus Christ.

❧ Bibliography ❧

Alford, Henry, *The Greek Testament*, Boston, MA: Lee and Shepard Publishers, 1878

Arndt, W., Gingrich, F. W., *A Greek-English Lexicon of the New Testament and Other Early Christian Literature*, Chicago, IL: University of Chicago Press, 1957

Barnhouse, Donald Grey, *The Invisible War*, Grand Rapids, MI: Zondervan Publishing House, 1965

Barnes, Albert, *Notes on the New Testament*, Grand Rapids, MI: Baker Books, 14 Vols, 2005

Bloesch, Donald G., *Essentials of Evangelical Theology*, Peabody, MA: Prince Press, 2001

Brown, Colin, Ed., *New International Dictionary of New Testament Theology*, Grand Rapids, MI: Zondervan Publishing House, 1986

Calvin, J., & Beveridge, H., *Institutes of the Christian Religion*, Peabody, MA: Hendrickson, 2009

Chafer, Lewis Sperry, *Systematic Theology*, Dallas, TX: Dallas Seminary Press, 8 Vols., 1976

_____. *The Epistle to the Ephesians*, Grand Rapids, MI: Kregel, 1991

_____. *Salvation: God's Marvelous Work of Grace*, Grand Rapids, MI: Kregel, 1991

_____. *Major Bible Themes*, Grand Rapids, MI: Zondervan Publishing House, 1974

_____. *He That Is Spiritual,* Grand Rapids, MI: Zondervan Publishing House, 1967

Couch, Mal, Ed., *The Fundamentals for the Twenty-First Century,* Grand Rapids, MI: Kregel, 2000

Cowper, William, "Exhortation to Prayer," *The Works of the Rev. John Newton,* New Haven, CT: Nathan Whiting, 1826

Cubberly, Ellwood P., *Public Education in the United States,* Boston, MA: Houghton Mifflin, 1919

Easton, M., *Easton's Bible Dictionary,* Oak Harbor, WA: Logos Research Systems, Inc., 1996

Gaebelein, Frank E., Ed., *The Expositor's Bible Commentary,* Grand Rapids, MI: Zondervan Publishing House, 12 Vols., 1979

Geisler, Norman L., *Systematic Theology,* Minneapolis, MN: Bethany House, 4 Vols., 2002

_____. *Christian Apologetics,* Peabody, MA: Prince Press, 2003

Getz, Gene A., *Sharpening the Focus of the Church,* Chicago, IL: Moody Press, 1976

Henry, Matthew, *Matthew Henry's Commentary on the Whole Bible,* New York, NY: Fleming H. Revell, 6 Vols., n/d

Hodge, Charles, *Systematic Theology,* Peabody, MA: Hendrickson, 3 Vols., 2001

_____. *Commentary on the Epistle to the Romans,* Albany, OR: AGES Software, 1997

The Holy Bible: English Standard Version, Wheaton, IL: Crossway Bibles, 2001

Jamieson, R., Fausset, A. R., & Brown, D., *A Commentary, Critical and Explanatory, on the Old and New Testaments.* On spine: Critical and Explanatory Commentary (electronic edition), Oak Harbor, WA: Logos Research Systems, Inc., 1997

Lenski, R.C.H., *Commentary on the New Testament,* Peabody, MA: Hendrickson, 12 Vols., 2001

Lewis, C. S., *Mere Christianity*, SanFransico, CA: Harper Collins, 2001

MacDonald, W., & Farstad, A., *Believer's Bible Commentary: Old and New Testaments* (electronic ed.) Nashville, TN: Thomas Nelson, 1997

Metzger, Bruce M., *A Textual Commentary on the Greek New Testament*, Stuttgart: United Bible Societies, 2001

The Nelson Study Bible: New King James Version, Nashville, TN: Thomas Nelson Publishers, 1997

New American Standard Bible: 1995 Update. La Habra, CA: The Lockman Foundation

Original Languages Library, Oak Harbor, WA: Logos Research Systems, Inc.

Pentecost, J. Dwight, *Things to Come*, Grand Rapids, MI: Zondervan Publishing House, 1964

Ramm, Bernard, *Protestant Biblical Interpretation*, Boston, MA: W.A. Wilde Company, 1956

Robertson, A.T., *Word Pictures in the New Testament*, Nashville, TN: Broadman Press, 6 Vols., 1931

_____. *A Grammar of the Greek New Testament in the Light of Historical Research*, Nashville, TN: Broadman Press, 1934

Ryrie, Charles C., *The Ryrie Study Bible*: Expanded Edition, NASB, Chicago, IL: Moody Press, 1995

_____. *Dispensationalism*, Chicago, IL: Moody Press, 1995

_____. *Balancing the Christian Life*, Chicago, IL: Moody Press, 1970

Schaff, Philip, *History of the Christian Church*. Peabody, MA: Hendrickson, 8 Vols., 2006

_____. *The Nicene and Post-Nicene Fathers, Second Series*, Albany, OR: The Ages Digital Library Collection, 1997

Schaeffer, Francis A., *The Complete Works of Francis A. Schaeffer*, Wheaton, IL: Crossway Books, 5 Vols., 1985

Scofield, C. I., *The Scofield Study Bible*, New York, NY: Oxford University Press, 1957

Strauss, Lehman, *The Book of the Revelation*, Neptune, NJ: Loizeaux Brothers, 1985

Unger, Merrill F., *Principles of Expository Preaching*, Grand Rapids, MI: Zondervan Publishing House, 1977

Unger, Merrill F., *The New Unger's Bible Dictionary*, Chicago, IL: Moody Press, 1988

Van Ryn, August, *The Epistles of John*, New York, NY: Loizeaux Brothers, 1948

Van Til, Cornelius, *The Defense of the Faith*, Phillipsburg, NJ: Presbyterian and Reformed Publishing Co., 1967

Vine, W. E., *Collected Writings of W.E. Vine* (electronic ed.). Nashville, TN: Thomas Nelson, 5 Vols., 1996

Vine, W. E., Unger, M. F., & White, W., *Vine's Complete Expository Dictionary of Old and New Testament Words*, Nashville, TN: Thomas Nelson, 1996

Wallace, D. B., *Greek Grammar Beyond the Basics*: An Exegetical Syntax of the Greek New Testament, Grand Rapids, MI: Zondervan Publishing House, 1996

Webster's Seventh New Collegiate Dictionary, Springfield, MS: G & C Merriam Company, 1965

The Westminster Confession of Faith, Oak Harbor, WA: Logos Research Systems, Inc., 1996

Wood, D. R. W., & Marshall, I. H., *New Bible Dictionary* (3rd ed.), Leicester, England; Downers Grove, IL: InterVarsity Press, 1996

Wuest, K. S., *Wuest's Word Studies from the Greek New Testament*: For the English reader, Grand Rapids: Eerdmans, 4 Vols., 1998

Youngblood, R. F., *Nelson's New Illustrated Bible Dictionary* (F. F. Bruce, Ed.) (Electronic ed. of the revised ed. of Nelson's illustrated Bible dictionary.) Nashville, TN: Thomas Nelson, 1997

Zodhiates, Spiros, *The Complete Word Study Dictionary: New Testament* (electronic ed.) Chattanooga, TN: AMG Publishers, 2000